The Joy
of Running
qua Running

The Joy
of Running
qua Running

An ode in twenty poems, thirty-six short essays, and
one logical proof dubious in both soundness and validity.

SCOTT F. PARKER

INSIDE THE CURTAIN PRESS

Books by the same author: *Running after Prefontaine: A Memoir*; *Run for Your Life: A Manifesto*; *Being on the Oregon Coast*; *A Way Home: Oregon Essays*; *in series* (writing as the Synthesis); and others. He is the editor of *Conversations with Joan Didion*; *Conversations with Ken Kesey*; *Eminem and Rap, Poetry, Race*; and *Coffee—Philosophy for Everyone: Grounds for Debate* (with Mike W. Austin).

Some of the pieces in this book appeared previously, sometimes in different form and/or under different title: "Run the Numbers" and "Deduction on the Run" at *Mathematical Runner*; "Runners at Play" in the *Bozeman Daily Chronicle* as "Cross Cut 25K: Runners at Play"; "The Joy of Running qua Running," "On the Trail with Donald Porter," "On My Feet," "Runner on the Road!," "Run Away," "Watching Boston," and "I Like this Poem" in *Sport Literate*; "Dispatches from the Wild Rogue Relay" in the *Oregonian* under other titles; "Meet Me in Eugene," "Better than Okay," "Not Even to the River Yet," and the review of *Two Hours* in *Run Minnesota*; the review of *Running with the Pack* in *Philosophy Now*; "Why Run?" at *Uproxx* as "Even the Rainy Days"; "Cross Country Season" in *bosque*; "How to Lose a Toenail in Style," "Running with the Stars," and "An Oral History of Joe Parker, Self-Described Hood to Coast Legend, by Those Who Know Him Well" in *Hood to Coast Memories*; and "On Newton Road" in *The Poeming Pigeon*.

About the author: according to Mark Remy's indispensable *Runners of North America: A Definitive Guide to the Species*, he is a hybrid subspecies of runner combining phenotypical traits of the 7:00-Minute-Mile Guy (*Lopus mono velocitus*), the Barefoot Runner (*Lopus naturalis*), and the Trail Runner (*Lopus granolus*). An alternative interpretation of the data contends that he is, rather, an immature member of the subspecies Grizzled Vet (*Lopus veteranus*). He leaves it to posterity to settle such disputes. He would like to take the opportunity here to express his opinion that dogs should be kept on leashes when city ordinance requires it (even if the City of Bozeman does not enforce this particular ordinance (Sec. 8.02.080.) with any reliability) and most of the time when there's no relevant ordinance on the books. It's common courtesy. Other miscellaneous opinions, observations, resolutions, and pleas: The author is practicing not hitting cars that nearly hit him as eagerly, as frequently, or as hard as he did when he was, let's just say, a teenager. Please read and support *Dumb Runner*, which is produced by the above-mentioned Mark Remy and is a brilliant example of how to love running and not take it too seriously. Any readers who are interested in starting (or funding) an online magazine to review running books and eventually branch out to feature other genres of running-related writing, please contact the author at scottfparker@gmail.com. In light of the recent (not to mention the not-so-recent) scandals plaguing Nike (which after fifteen years in Frees the author now joins good people like the ever-exemplary Kara Goucher in boycotting), he proudly joins the chorus asking: WWPreD? Finally, the author would like squeeze in a brief account of a runner he witnessed just before this book went to press. He and his wife were walking in the woods this morning. The ground was thick with snow. A runner passed, taking tiny steps. They didn't hear her coming. Her feet hardly touched the ground. She left no trace. Had the wind had been blowing, it would have passed right through her. If you told the author that he'd imagined her he'd almost believe you.

THIS BOOKS IS FOR COACH KATIE

ISBN: 978-0-9839562-3-5

The right way to run is by dancing.
—Alan Watts

CONTENTS

THE JOY OF RUNNING QUA RUNNING

ABSTRACT

r u n
n i n g
a n d
t h e
m e a n
i n g
o f
l i f e
a n d
o t h
e r
o f
f e r
i n g s
f o r
f r i e n d s

RUN THE NUMBERS

1. The first-person: *I*. The will, the self, the subject of the experience of all those miles all those miles all those mornings all those trails all those routes all those repeats all those shoes all those blisters all those recoveries all those stretches all those runs. The experience of running is always private.

2. Legs. There's not much else you need run.

3. The holy running trinity of body, mind, and soul—unified not in every run but in enough runs.

4. Minutes. And everything it still connotes.

5. Kilometers to measure yourself, to find out if you will ever run faster than you ran at seventeen. You haven't yet.

7. The threshold in miles at which the possibility of a long run becomes conceivable.

11. Teammates on your Hood to Coast team (as long as your cousin Zach doesn't drop out at the last minute for no good reason).

13.1. The bumper sticker you're better off not putting on your car.

15. American records set by Steve Prefontaine.

23. Temperature (Fahrenheit) below which running isn't really worth it.

25. Ground miles (approximate) from Marathon to Athens.

36. Age at which you give up all contact sports, hoping to increase your chances of forty-plus running years ahead.

42 – 50. The ideal length (in minutes) of a leisurely run on a nice day.

94. Age at which Harriette Thompson became the oldest person to run a half-marathon.

100. Chance (in percentage) that what it means for your favorite professional to run is not what it means for you to run.

160.524. Miles Patrycja Bereznowska ran in twenty-four hours.

300 – 500. Miles they say a pair of running shoes is good for. (If you've been running in the same pair since 2009 and feel fine, don't sweat it.)

1,500. A cruel distance (in meters) to race. Masochistic, frankly.

10,000. Sometimes more than, sometimes less than, but never equal to, twice 5,000 (meters), depending on the day.

33,000. Average number of strides per marathon.

50,000+. Finishers in the New York City Marathon.

∞. The thing we're all the time chasing with these miles we're running.

RUNNERS AT PLAY

DISTANCE RUNNING ISN'T A SPORT, it's a personality trait. A runner can no more cease to run than he can cease to be, as the mold enjoins, concentrated, self-possessed, and inclined toward the comforts of routine. What non-runners don't always recognize in the runner is that his primary experience, of which running is the physical expression, is of playfulness. A runner is never freer than when his stride is playing the metronomic rhythm to which his spirit may improvise.

Four, five, when the weather is nice seven times a week, I tie up my running shoes and head out the front door or get in the car and drive myself to the woods. For forty-five minutes or an hour and a half I report only to my mood and my energy.

When I was younger I thought of running as something I did, in the same way that I played basketball and listened to music. But as you age you learn that certain parts of you are essential and that these must be protected against the forces of adult complacency. I could deny myself this exercise, but it would be dishonest and self-destructive to do so.

By now, in my thirties, my legs increasingly take their time to loosen up. I start out slow the first mile, something I never did in my twenties. My legs are smarter than whatever it is I call *I* and they'll pick up the pace as it's time. Much wisdom resides in the body. At those times when the prospects of my life feel most hopeless or the simple frustration of not knowing what the next sentence is wears a rut in my consciousness, running returns me to a saner version of myself.

I signed up for the Cross Cut 25K in the Bridger Range of southwest Montana on a bit of a whim. I've always enjoyed the experience of racing, but I haven't done as much of it over the past few years as I did in the past. What's more, I have never cared enough about results to design, let alone follow, a proper training regimen. Who but myself, I have always figured, in the full contingency of my existence on this one day and course, am I racing?

But there I was at the Jim Bridger Lodge at 7 a.m. on Saturday, lined up with the kind of sinewy, shaved-leg men and women you just don't see too many of at your neighborhood 5K. The moon was heavy over the Bridgers, and the air still snappy at mountain dawn.

One of the strategies I've learned from long races is to settle as quickly as possible into the pace at which I exert no effort. It might be six or eight or twelve minutes per mile, but every runner has such a pace. Once there, running becomes less a race than an exercise in patience. If I can rest in that place the finish line will come to me. I've never been in good enough shape to really race a marathon, but I can usually relax through the first twenty miles and grit through the last six-point-two. But climbing makes that approach impractical. The only way up Bridger Bowl is one step at a time.

I felt good putting one foot in front of the other straight up the ski hill. Soon, I fell in with a group of similarly proficient runners in file through the tight turns of the single-track trail. Had I been alone I would have stopped here and there to appreciate the view and felt the wave of vertigo that attends a big Montana vista. Instead, I kept my eyes on the ground and focused on identifying a safe landing for each footfall, especially as we crested the first long climb and began a not insignificant descent.

Of course, not all who run are runners. For some a run is a sacrifice made at the altar of thinness. For others, such as the guy immediately in front of me for some of the race's early miles, it is something from which distraction is apparently required. Here we are in the quiet morning woods, and here he is with his earbuds so loud other runners can't get his attention to pass without reaching out to tap him on the shoulder. I am reminded at such moments that runners are those for whom the ends and the means of the activity align, and for whom running isn't an escape into a private world but a way of being in this one.

At the second water station the 15K and 25K courses split apart, and I spent the next long stretch of miles mostly alone. In retrospect, this was the flat part of the race, but only because up gave way to down and vice versa in quick succession. I rolled over dips and hillocks, through forests and meadows, with ease and contentment.

That was, until, the third water station. I asked the attendant there how far into the race we were. He didn't know. I supposed about ten miles, maybe eleven, as I set out on what would be a long, and for me demanding, climb over the next four miles or so. The mountain suddenly felt indomitable, given the reserves I had access to. This wasn't the pure muscle burning of a 5K when you're trying to redline as long as possible without collapsing. This was the basic struggle of being captive to the warring impulses of wanting to quit and knowing you can't. It's as fruitless as it is unavoidable. You go on.

The two courses converged for the last few miles and I passed a struggling 15K runner, who said to me, "Whoever made this course is a sadist."

I obliged her gallows humor by completing the joke, "Which must make us masochists," but, really, the runner's relationship with pain is more refined than that.

While we might harbor the belief that pain tolerance is a moral virtue somewhere in our psyches, we don't actually enjoy the pain of running; what we enjoy is the peace of mind that comes in knowing that we can withstand pain without undue suffering. We voluntarily enter a state of pain and hold ourselves there as long as it takes, never doubting that all the while we are in a profound sense *fine*. Pain is impermanent, and suffering is optional.

When that last long climb reached its apex, the course dropped straight down the face of Bridger Bowl in what the organizers, who probably are sadists after all, refer to as a "quad burner." The sole objective at this point was not to tumble down the mountain.

I was tired and I was hurting and I was still on my feet. And like so many others I was right where I wanted to be.

TOP TEN

YOU SIGN UP FOR YOUR first official race. You are nine. You are probably as fast as Carl Lewis. Or at least on your way to being. Have you ever known someone faster than you? Maybe Andrew from soccer. But only him. And you'll beat him next season. How far is a mile? Not far. You'll probably win. Probably start running track afterward. Probably make the Olympic team when you're twenty. The race is along the waterfront. Half a mile north. Turnaround. Half a mile back south to the finish. You have your tennis shoes on. Why are they called tennis shoes you like to ask your mom if you wear them for everything and only play tennis a few times a summer. It would make more sense to call them basketball shoes or running shoes or tree-climbing shoes since that's what they do way more of. That's just what they're called, she says. Which illogic hasn't yet ceased to amuse you. Adults really aren't very bright. Nevertheless, you've got your tennis shoes on and the shorts you wear to soccer practice and a white T-shirt and you would have worn a headband if you'd found one because it would have made you look as fast as everyone is probably about to find out you are. Your race bib is pinned to the front of your shirt and you should either be careful with that because it will probably need to go in a museum one day or be reckless with it so that when it ends up in that museum one day it'll look like it's really been through some stuff. Something heroic. The race is starting. There are fifty or a hundred or five hundred runners in your age category. You take your place at the front. Your mom said to pace yourself, but your mom doesn't know a thing about running.

She's never raced you farther than to like the corner and didn't even beat you when you were all of six let alone now. She doesn't know can't possibly know what it's like for you to propel your body through space with such velocity such exuberance that if you were thinking you might be thinking about how good you feel and how your problems are so far away they likely won't ever catch you again or how strain is the feeling of overcoming or how a person can be his own hero or how will is the force of life or any of the other things that are perfectly obvious to anyone who has run a little bit faster than he's able. But you're not thinking. There's no time for thinking. No time at all. Your feelings aren't getting turned into ideas. They're just being felt. And when you look back you'll know that the feeling was good. It was the feeling of being young and alive and, I ask you not to be afraid of this word, *happy*. It doesn't matter that despite your best effort you couldn't maintain a sprint for the whole mile. It doesn't matter that you got tenth. It doesn't matter that you'll never join the track team. It doesn't matter that you won't make the Olympic team. None of that matters. What matters is the experience and the accessibility of it and the reliability of it and the taste of it. You are nine years old. You are not as fast today as the nine kids who beat you. You are not nearly as fast as Carl Lewis. But you are fast enough.

CROSS COUNTRY SEASON

i remember the first day of practice and wondering if i was fast, if i could keep up, if i belonged.

i remember butterflies in my belly & cement in my legs.

i remember the ripe smell of the jersey my coach pulled out of the locker as he had for twenty years of runners before me.

i remember thinking the shorts were too short for me to look cool in front of girls.

i remember our coach talking to the boys team about the versatility of duct tape.

i remember golden sunlight & late summer evenings that faded like a kiss.

i remember getting a little drunk the night before a morning practice in the summer and feeling like i'd never been so alive.

i remember the wonder of running in Forest Park that first summer.

i remember fresh sweat smelling good on people i liked, sometimes even myself.

i remember that the girls' shorts were short too.

i remember bus rides to away meets and the expansive feeling of camaraderie.

i remember the nervous energy of youth and the flirting it facilitated before a race.

i remember Saturday morning long runs with members of the girls team.

i remember fall wind and the stillness of Portland air before rain.

i remember early morning runs alone in the dark.

i remember new neighborhoods and new eyes.

i remember that insecurity is one of many things one doesn't have to carry on the run.

i remember the drizzle and the cold and the shower after.

i remember that no one in the school really cared about cross country and that it didn't matter.

i remember feeling proud at the alumni meet my uncle ran with me.

i remember the routes we ran at practice week after week. (i still run them when i'm home.)

i remember every nuance of our home course, when to be ready for a tricky tree root, when to catch an opponent off guard with a burst of speed, when to look poised for the crowd.

i remember how my body felt by the middle of the season: tired, well used, powerful, and loved.

i remember how easily our coach could be moved to tears or enthusiasm and admiring him for it.

i remember his recruiting motto—"Run for fun!"—and the mocking it only sort of deserved.

i remember he didn't have kids of his own.

i remember being too young for my own opportunities and kinda knowing it and not being too concerned, all things considered.

i remember training hard enough.

i remember thinking a 5K was a substantial undertaking and then volunteering at the Portland Marathon.

i remember occasionally surprising myself during a race.

i remember fear and confidence and excitement and restraint competing in their own race.

i remember elbows in the pack the first quarter mile.

i remember being alone in the race, but not entirely.

i remember the body-sick of the finish line.

i remember beating a runner i didn't know i could and losing to one i didn't think i would.

i remember setting my PR in my final race and feeling sad.

i remember the feeling i had when i was running that i could go wherever i wanted.

GIVE IT YOUR BEST

GENTLEMEN, . . . MY legs feel alright. That's good. . . . *there is honor to sport.* . . . How's my stomach? Did I eat enough? Did I eat too much? . . . *There is the honor of victory, yes,* . . . Am I hydrated? Overhydrated? . . . *and of hard work and camaraderie and sportsmanship, absolutely.* . . . Should I go out fast or start easy? . . . *But there is an honor that lies deeper even than these.* . . . Double knot your shoes. Take a deep breath. Relax. . . . *It is the honor of being.* . . . My best time isn't really that good when you stop to think about all the people who can run faster. . . . *Running reveals the ethic and aesthetic layered not atop but within the brute physical fact of a race.* . . . If I could run faster people would be impressed. . . . *Gentlemen,* . . . That would be something. . . . *pursue the limits of yourselves.* . . . Maybe I'd be happier and enjoy life more. . . . *You are as you run.* . . . I could go to California and be chill and hang out with girls. . . . *So run fast.* . . . What is my worth as a human being if I do not succeed in my endeavors? . . . *Run to glory, run to triumph,* . . . And how can success be a relative term? . . . *to run is to expand yourselves.* . . . I should have trained more over the summer, done more long runs and put more effort into my speed work. . . . *Burst forth, my boys! What is great is inside you.* . . . I wish I could turn back time. I could really get this stuff right the second time around. . . . *Your power is your spirit.* . . . There's that one song that goes I wish I knew what I know now when I was younger. That pretty much gets at it. . . . *When you grow you become yourselves.* . . . But I could have anticipated that I'd later wish I had trained more. . . . *Become yourselves, boys!* . . . The problem is I didn't want to train more at the time. . . . *Become men!* . . . And why should I have let the me of today control the me of the summer? . . . *Live! Expand! Flourish!* . . . Now this me just has to accept things as they are. . . . *Run and run and* . . . If I am ashamed of myself it is the same I that feels the shame. . . . *by what is holy in your bones* . . . There's that knot of identity I can't untie. . . . *may you run your best!*

CURRO ERGO SUM

TWO THINGS HAPPENED JUNIOR YEAR of high school that have stuck with me in ways I could not have anticipated. First, I took up running. Second, I started reading philosophy. For twenty years I've maintained both activities, but it's only now that I'm starting to wonder how they might be related.

I went out for cross country that fall in order to spend more time around a girl I liked, to burn off the calories I was sure were keeping me from happiness, and as one of the big steps in the larger project of redirecting the course of my life after two lackluster years of high school. Taken together (and surely they were more tangled in the stuff of me than delineating them here suggests), these motivations indicate a clear overarching desire to transform the self I had been into the one I wanted to be.

Philosophy came to me the following spring and quite by accident. I stumbled upon Plato's theory of forms in the course of writing an essay about beauty for English class. Beauty itself didn't interest me particularly, but the way Plato thought rang absolute bells. What do beautiful instances share such that, various as they are, we recognize beauty as common to them? Right away I wanted to generalize even further: how do our ideas about the world relate to the world itself?

I understood from the start that I had been taking philosophy personally long before I knew what philosophy was. What Plato offered was a language in which I could think about the forces that were already welling up inside me that year. To come right to the point of why I was running: I wanted to know to what degree it was in my power to compel change self-reflexively.

If I was constantly changing, who or what was I? If I could shape who I was, who or what was shaping the I that did that shaping? How did how other people saw me affect how I saw myself, and how did each of these relate to who I really was? If some people did not wonder about such things, why not, and which of us was better off? If asking such questions did keep me from happiness, should I—could I—quit asking them? Perhaps all of these questions and other variations of them could be subsumed under the abiding question, *What is the self?* Or, because it's always felt personally, *Who or what am I?*

Running, as it turned out, did and did not transform me. The girl I liked became one of the dearest friends I'd ever known. I counted that relationship a fortune, even if we never figured out how to be a couple. My obsession with calories would stay with me three more years, but in the short term the fact that running did burn a lot of them brought me a certain kind of happiness. As for the project of redirecting my life generally, running showed me that I could put myself into new situations and thrive; I learned that I liked running, that I was faster than I'd realized, and that new pursuits allowed me to experience new parts of myself in new company. But at the center of those experiences, as I was a little surprised and a little disappointed to find, I was still pretty much the same old me. Disappointed because the goal, after all, hadn't been to change my life in order to have a different life. It had been to change my life in order to become a different person. What went wrong?

Skip ahead twenty years. I no longer have the acute desire for self-reinvention. So what do I run for now? Why have I kept up running all these years?

First and last, it brings me joy, and one of the orienting convictions of my adulthood has been that things that bring joy are worth pursuing in their own right. In the case of running, the joy is a generalized well-being comprising some combination of mental clarity, emotional lift, and physical pleasure. And underlying this sense of well-being is a deeper—and for me precious—sense of personal congruence. It is as if running allows me to be who I am.

This works, I have come to believe, only as long as I don't run *in order to* gain mental clarity, emotional lift, or physical pleasure. I have learned that the rewards of running are inseparable from the act of running. So instead of running for instrumental reasons, no matter how high minded, I have kept up running because it feels right to me. Making sense of that feeling comes only later, when I determine that the mental clarity, emotional lift, and physical pleasure that attend running are byproducts of that deeper congruence that comes with expressing who I really am.

It is the congruence that I think matters more than running itself. My account is not exhaustive. I am not claiming that running is the only way I can be myself or that running necessarily makes me myself. All I'm doing is noticing that very often running does make me feel like myself. And from the point of view of someone who once thought it of dire importance to become someone else, this is saying quite a bit indeed.

This felt congruence bears an abstract implication. When I run I'm not troubled by the problems of selfhood. The paradoxes of identity and self-consciousness vanish. And not in the sense that when you don't think about a problem it's as if the problem ceases to exist. They vanish in a way more like seeing that a problem itself was based on a confusion that has been resolved. There is no longer a problem either to address or ignore. Perhaps this is due to our species having evolved as runners or to physical exertion suppressing discursive thought or to running's capacity to yoke mind and body or to something else still. It doesn't matter why running can produce this sense of being myself, only that it can.

The most straightforward way I know to dispatch Descartes's *Cogito ergo sum* is to notice that it begs the question. Rather than *I think,* what one actually observes upon introspection is *thinking* (not to mention, sometimes *not-thinking*). And if you eliminate the I who thinks, what remains? *Thinking therefore thinking* doesn't have quite the same ring to it. If we're going to establish the certainty of self, we need to do better than summon it out of grammar.

I propose running on experiential, not intellectual, grounds. I can't clinch this argument beyond doubt, nor would I attempt to. I have no quest for certainty. My only quest is for well-being, which is the bounty running delivers.

Do I mean it, then? *Curro ergo sum?*

"I" is an impossible thought. As soon as I try to think it, I am divided from it. The subject is made an object in language. But something like "I" is not an impossible experience. A flower doesn't strive to be a bird. It's perfectly flower as long as it exists. A similar experience is available to us. It is the state of doing what is in one's nature, the state of willing only oneself. It is a state of whole-self absorption that I've spent my life chasing and that I've approached most reliably on the run. The experiential grounds are these: Running is a way of being in the world. It is active. It is engaged. It is spontaneous. It is responsive. It is mental. It is physical. It is emotional. It might even be spiritual. And in all of this the self it figures is unified in a way even the most absorbed cognition can never allow. It's not that running does what philosophy can't. It's that running is philosophy. At least it's the kind of philosophy I'm interested in: the kind that expands you and allows you to become who you are.

If I could go back twenty years and meet the boy who wanted so desperately to become someone else, I'd tell him he already was and he always would be. I would not tell him that the more he ran the more he would see this was the truth. I'd want to let him figure that out for himself.

I LIKE THIS POEM

I get it. It's not like those ones in school
Where the teacher asks if you can identify
All the metaphors for God or democracy
Or whatever. What is a metaphor anyway?

And why can't a poem just be about
Whatever it's about, like this one,
Which is about running. I get running.
Everyone knows what running is.

So when the poet says running
We all know what he's talking about
And we know that it just means running
And not some other thing about mortality

Or the will to power or anything
Hifalutin like that. Running is running.
That's it. And there's no reason on earth
To make it any more complicated than that.

THANK YOU

ON VACATION TWENTY YEARS AFTER graduating high school I bumped into my cross country coach in an art gallery featuring his woodwork. "Hey, Coach," I said. "Help me out," he said. I wasn't surprised he didn't remember me. A little disappointed, I admit, but not surprised. I was an unremarkable runner, just fast enough to squeeze into the team's top seven and run varsity, but not good enough to challenge for wins or usually score for the team (finish in the top five). Factor in decades of such runners and dozens faster and hundreds, maybe thousands, slower, factor in age, factor in twenty years being a long time—it would be shocking, I tell myself, if he did remember me. Of course, the concern of this essay so far betrays my desire to have been so shocked. Didn't part of me want to have made a lasting impression on the sport that made such a profound impact on me. But that's just the ego complaining. The point isn't to be recognized. The point is to be grateful. The point is to express gratitude in the appropriate circumstance. Like when you see your first and only running coach and tell him that twenty years ago you could not have seen twenty years into the future but that if you could have you like to think you'd have been happy. Because that's what running does for you more than just about anything else: makes you happy. And after twenty years you're still running. And you hope to be running for forty more. And anyone who played a role in that deserves a healthy share of your gratitude. So, thank you, Coach Cotton. Thank you for miles.

COUNCIL CREST, PORTLAND RAIN

STARTING OUT FROM YOUR PARENTS' house, where you've started a thousand runs before, you greet the December rain like an old friend offering a hug. You can't get any wetter than you already are and as long as you stay moving you won't get too cold. You pass the places you always pass, this house and that one, where your childhood friends lived—and sometimes your enemies—this street where you found out how strong you were and that street where you found out strong you weren't, ultimately glad to know both. You reach the river. You've always been fond of winter rain on the river. And so you cross slowly with your gaze aimed downriver like you could almost follow this weather system to the ocean. You could turn around here. It would make for a nice run: to the river and back. But something today draws you across the water. How far you don't know yet but it feels like the farther you run the farther there is left in this run. Sometimes it works this way. So you continue through downtown and south across the university's campus toward the base of the highest hill in the city. It is raining harder now, rain drops stinging on exposed skin. You wonder what you're doing running this far in this weather. What exactly is the plan here? But you know the plan. You'll climb to the top. You won't stop until there's nowhere left to go, and from there you'll have no choice but to make it back. How many miles are we talking here? Twelve? Fourteen? That sounds right, give or take. The miles aren't a problem. In fact, look around, there is no problem. The world is full of people carrying out little missions they've invented for themselves as their circumstances allow. Most of these missions you'll be ignorant of your whole life. But here you are on one of your own: to Council Crest and back in a terrific rain for no reason whatsoever. You can disappear inside this kind of project. And what about the paradox that as long as you commit yourself to this run you will have the most perfect freedom you've ever known. Only stopping or wishing it weren't raining or worrying about getting cold or tired, only these can restrict you. Be wet, be cold, be tired, be free. You run on the sloppy park trails to the top of the city. You reach the summit and see gray on gray on gray on everything that isn't a tree. There's no view to take in and no time to take it for the runner who doesn't stop but turns back around and follows Vista to Burnside to Broadway to Seventh to Thompson to his parents' home where he is wet and cold and tired and feeling like he has a secret that everyone on this Earth should want to want for themselves because on this day for these hours he has known exactly what he was doing by watching himself do it and finding out and maybe you live this way already and aren't affected by it but maybe you aren't and then you should be and could be and miles are nothing and rain is nothing and a hill is nothing and even running is nothing and you are nothing too or you can be sometimes if you're lucky.

ON NEWTON ROAD

Yesterday I ran in the woods of my youth,
enjoying the sweet hush of solitude
while the dense foliage of green summer
swelled all around me. Am I sentimental
or simply honest when I observe life
for a little while doing what it's supposed to?
The reason I run is as old as my bones.
There are mountain lions in these woods.
And bears. Mysteries loud and quiet. Perhaps
my legs have been initiated over years of miles
into this particular forest and retain the traces
of secret teachings—the way the trail leans,
the way the trees tell their own stories, the way
the undergrowth flirts with obscenity. Perhaps
running here is a homecoming. But life being
what life is, by what promise do I measure
these moments that come not always—
sometimes——sometimes enough.

THE LANGUAGE OF THE RUN

after Sharon Olds

I have wanted excellence in the foot-race,
I have wanted my muscular legs and cardiovascular
      strength for speed
and my steady gaze and my hard bones and my unfaltering
      equilibrium
to move over ground with relentless ease
like Coburn or Kipchoge.

I have wanted that elemental grace, some achievement
worthy of my profound body, some human exceptionalism
to replace my all-too-human ability, my barely above-
      average
speed, my wholly particular self wanting to burst out, I
      have stood in the crowd
and watched the elites race by.

I have wanted desire, I have thought about pain
and the disregard for limits, I have made do with

the stitch in my side,
the rock in my shoe and the blister on my foot,
my breath wheezy and gasping,
my lungs burning, legs pleading,
my face crystaled with salt, thighs
and nipples chafed raw like meat, my mind
tired and depleted like a worn-out sock.
I have stopped.

I have stopped and rested and resumed
and struggled and shaken and continued and
slowly alone in the center of experience I have
ceased to recognize any difference
between running and not running, between
my body and myself and anything else that
might arise in the language of the run.

I have done what you wanted me to do,
Steve Prefontaine, I have done this thing,
I and the other runners, this divine
enterprise for this divine creature,
this exercise, practice, this human being human,
and I am vanishing like you and
like everyone else after the race
        is run.

A SHORT ESSAY ON SOME LOCAL RUNNERS,
BLESS THEM ALL

FOR INSTANCE, THE FORTY-FIVE-YEAR-OLD MAN who was at every race I ran when I was starting out twenty years ago, who rumor had it ran two races every weekend year round and fact had it never beat me by less than three minutes, even in a 5K, and who as far as we know is still forty-five, still running two races a weekend, and still faster than I'll ever be;

the woman with water bottles strapped to her body as to survive a week in the Sahara while she jogs slowly around our suburb;

the girl coming toward me easily on a park trail whose record-setting results I read about only last week in the newspaper and wouldn't otherwise recognize as anything other than one of us;

the old man who could walk as fast as he's running but is running anyway;

the college student whose main goal appears to be running at the rate of maximum effort that will not have her break a sweat and soil her cute outfit or cause her designer sunglasses to slide from the bridge of her nose;

the New Year's Resolution runners who won't be out here tomorrow but are out here today; and also today, the polar plungers, who will be out here next year too;

the girl with the long socks, the guy with no socks, and the poor young man down to one sock;

the every-three-hundred-miles-a-new-pair-of-shoes runner, the barefoot runner, the extra-padding extra-support extra-everything runner, the whatever-shoes-I-happened-to-put-on runner, the-these-are-fine runner, the can-we-please-not-talk-about-running-shoes-ever-again-my-god-enough-already runner;

the middle-aged man with diarrhea running down his leg as he navigates the busy neighborhood back to his home passing friends and strangers along the way, every stride replete with dignity;

the lopers, the grinders, the bouncers, even the breathers, the sweaters, the stinkers, the overdressed and the underprepared, the ambitious and the cautious;

the one you can just tell is completely new to this and will be stiff as a corpse tomorrow;

the one who has run herself ragged today, and the one who never will;

the one who embraces pain, and the one who fears it, as well as the one who thinks in other terms;

the guy who looks like a clucking chicken the way he bobs his head in a rhythm I can't discern and flails his elbows like wings that won't fly and somehow still looks like he's having the time of his life day after day;

the one who surged to try and prevent me from passing him (never her) even as we were the only two people on our particular trail in the woods;

the one who really believes he's only doing it for his dog's benefit;

the one who, by god, will get herself ready for this marathon even if she never runs again;

the office worker who is pleased to make the acquaintance of the body that has been with him all along;

the two friends who talked themselves into it—and are having a nice time on this pleasant afternoon, wouldn't you agree;

bless them, bless them all;

even the ones wearing earbuds;

even the ones stuck on treadmills—

running is the invitation we've all accepted.

BETTER THAN OKAY

RUNNERS, PUT DOWN YOUR GADGETS and step away from the internet.

Don't worry. You'll be okay for an hour without it.

Excuse me for saying so, but I think early in 2015, more than ever, we can use a reminder that the only technology running requires is what you're born with. Maybe you put on a pair of shoes and, if you're in Minnesota as I am, layer up to protect against the cold. But that's about it.

I offer this reminder after reading in a recent issue of *Runner's World* that 96 percent of runners now use electronic technology of some kind.

That number sounds high to me. And it's not merely a case of no one I know voting for Nixon. In fact, many, even most, of my friends do run with headphones and various other cords to connect things with buttons to press and beeps to attend to and so on. It's not even that when I run by the lakes near my home many more than 4 percent of runners I cross paths with appear without electronic augmentation.

It's that *Runner's World* speaks for and to the running lifestyle more than the running experience. On every one of its pages, *Runner's World* sells aspirations to runner-consumers. This is a hallmark of capitalism, to take a basic human activity and turn it into something that requires regular and sometimes significant expenditures. For a media outlet like *Runner's World*, this mood helps to ensure advertising revenue. But for the reader, it normalizes the inadequacy of self that consumerism requires: you are not okay unless you buy X, download Y, wear Z, and then, *please,* go on to promote it all on social media.

Even when *Runner's World* strikes a more low-tech tone, it finds a way to promote spending. Another recent issue said, "all it takes is a good pair of shoes and some wicking apparel to join our community." It doesn't sound like much, but already this is deeply exaggerated. I grew up running in Portland, rain capital of the running imagination, and I never once had wicking apparel for running, nor do I know what wicking apparel is. I wore shorts and a cotton T-shirt just like every other runner I knew. To this day, I swear by the shirt and shorts that are closest at hand.

To be fair to *Runner's World*, I came across these claims because I like the magazine enough to subscribe to it. My concern is not so much with them as with the implications of the culture they attest to.

By way of contrast, let me tell you about my run around Cedar Lake. It begins by tracing the northernmost finger of Lake of the Isles, the lake between where I live and Cedar. In the early summer there are yellow goslings there. Now it is winter and the lake is frozen and covered in snow. But if you listen you will still hear birds. As I leave Lake of the Isles I pass an elementary school, a restaurant, and a neighborhood bookstore I stop in sometimes. From there I turn onto a paved trail that follows an old train line. Crossing the Kenilworth Lagoon, where the kayakers have been replaced by cross-country skiers, this trail leads me to Cedar Lake. The first half follows a paved trail removed from traffic. I see fisherman and canoes in the summer, I pass cyclists and other runners. I see cardinals, turtles, crows, loons, and sometimes deer.

But it's for the east side of the lake that I run here. I turn off the paved lane and into the woods. Often I'll see other runners or walkers here, and fishermen. Just as often I'll be alone. At one particular spot I regularly pass through clouds of marijuana smoke and hear the sounds of teenage laughter. Once I saw a band filming a music video here, all the equipment brought in by bicycle. But mostly what I see is the light.

The way it glitters off the green leaves of summer. The way it slides in sideways on me in the winter. There is as much variety to the light and color as I care to notice—and the less distracted and preoccupied I am, the more I am able to.

Once I complete the lake I retrace my route through the Kenwood neighborhood and around Lake of the Isles and home. And here's the part I think matters: not ever have I said to myself, "That was nice. Now, if only I had had earbuds instead of birds and the rustling of tree leaves for my soundtrack"; or "Too bad the quantifiable details of my run won't automatically be tweeted out to all of my followers"; or "I hope when I stopped through the milkweed to give the lake breeze a clear shot at my forehead and feel the waning autumn sun on my chest it didn't disrupt the negative splits I wanted to achieve."

I could go on, but what this comes down to is a question of what running's for. Is it to improve speed? Is it to lose weight? Is it to prove oneself to others? It's possible to run for any of these reasons. And maybe fancy electronics can help with them. What I want to add is that it's possible to run for other reasons. It's possible to engage with running subjectively rather than reducing it to objective measurements of miles, pace, or calories. It's possible to attend to the experience of running—the freedom, the beauty, and the difficulty—rather than distract oneself from it with music and phones and data and all the rest. It's possible to interact consciously with your environment instead of isolating yourself from it. And it's possible that bringing your attention to your subjective experience of your environment is worthwhile. I won't say it's the only way to run, but I will encourage you, if not every time at least some of the time, to leave your digital life behind and step out into the world alone with your thoughts and experiences. It might be scary at first, but if you can give yourself a chance you'll find that it's possible to be okay with only the technology you were born with—maybe better than okay.

FEELING THE HEAT

I STUMBLED INTO THE UPSCALE chain grocery store and headed directly for the bathroom, where I sat down and shat volcanically for several minutes—long enough to hear multiple knocks at the door and inquiries of "How much longer you gonna be?"; long enough to convince myself there was no more to empty; and long enough to think back with a strange mixture of embarrassment, regret, and pride about how I'd gotten there.

Not two hours earlier I'd left my house with the "NEVER GIVE A INCH" spirit of Hank Stamper from Ken Kesey's *Sometimes a Great Notion* in me. Recalling what Kesey had said about his character—that he "knows that to stop fighting means to start dying"—I had prepared myself to venture out in the world and have a self-reliant, can-do, American experience. The plan was to run to the suburbs, around a lake, and back home (approx. 13 – 15 miles) on unshaded pavement in the heat of the Midwestern summer day.

Getting to and around the lake proved if not pleasant at least not unpleasant. Cruising along on the way back, though, things turned quickly wrong. A distance runner learns to ignore the voices in his head enticing him to stop, but when the demands for a break come from the legs it's a different story—and in this case I stopped running before I realized I needed to. There I was, standing in the shade doing some light stretching, regrouping, coaching myself that there weren't but five or so miles remaining. And there I was five minutes later, sitting on the toilet, dripping sweat wildly while shivering, and having a hell of a time trying to decide what to do next.

Exiting the bathroom, I considered summoning the optimism to try for home even if it meant walking, but I was shaky and lost faith as I approached the heat. A cashier at this point asked me if I was okay, and after a too-long pause in which I thought about my wife and felt unfamiliarly helpless I eventually responded, "No. Not really."

The cashier, a runner, sat me down on a bench, handed me her phone to call my wife for a ride home, and went off to retrieve water, orange juice, and a banana—all of which I ingested ravenously. When my wife arrived, I took $5 and, feeling a good bit sturdier, said to the cashier, "You've been so kind. At least let me repay you."

"I won't hear of it," she said. "Get some rest and feel better."

On the drive home, accepting of what felt like my failure, and grateful for those who had offered their care, I reflected dreamily on the limits and the seductions of self-reliance. Lee, Hank's younger brother, offers one of the best-known lines in *Sometimes a Great Notion*: "Besides, there are some things that can't be the truth even if they *did* happen." What happened *did* happen. Whether it would become the truth would depend entirely on how it looked from the future, for which I remained eager.

THE JOY OF RUNNING QUA RUNNING

RECENTLY I HEARD SOMETHING IN an old Alan Watts lecture that made me question the way we talk about running. It seems to me that more often than not we talk about it in the way we talk about everything else—as another duty to be squeezed into our already busy and productive lives. You know the attitude: whether it's waking up early to get in three miles before work or running during the lunch break or stopping off at the gym to hit the treadmill on the way home, we must keep up with our responsibility to stay in shape (or, direr, to get in shape). Running is one more thing we *have to* do. It's one more thing that's *good for us.*

But what could be more absurd than running because it's good for us?

We're all dying all the time. Any decade now, each of us will be gone.

"True," these Good for Yous say, "but don't you know if you run you'll get an extra part of a decade added on at the end?"

I can't help but recall the old Woody Allen joke: *this food is terrible—and such small portions.* Who wants to do something they don't want to do in order to have more time in which to do things they don't want to do?

If running is good for us it's good in the way that breathing air and drinking water are good for us. No one ever said, "I've thought about it and I've decided to breathe some air." Or: "I reviewed the data and it would be wise for me to drink this water." No. We drink water because we're thirsty. We breathe air because as soon as we don't it's the only thing we want.

It is the same with running. You run because you need to,

because you can't imagine living without it, because it brings you joy.

And if you don't miss running the way you missing breathing and drinking, there's no reason you should.

ON THE TRAIL WITH DONALD PORTER

WE MIGHT CALL IT *FLOW* or the *runner's high* or *the joy of running.* Donald Porter calls it *inner running,* that feeling or cluster of feelings that arise with the force and profundity to make a runner a runner. While each of these terms carries its own flavor, they all privilege the runner's subjective experience above his or her objective achievements. A runner, from this kind of perspective, isn't someone who necessarily runs fast or far but someone who runs because running is a wonderful thing to do.

What distinguishes Porter's inner running is his explicit linking of running and meditation. When approached the right way, "Meditative running can enable you to drop whatever you're clutching for a short time—the beginning of permanent release. It can be a time of day to look at what's happening inside. A time of day to break your normal patterns of obsessive thought. A time to clean your mind, to wash your spirit. Inner running means running for the good feelings associated with it, running for happiness, for joy, for the fun of it."

For many runners this is a common feature of running, but it's one that rarely gets discussed. Luckily for the reader, Porter isn't squeamish around feelings. Running makes him a happier, even a *better*, person; it's no surprise that his enthusiasm for running becomes contagious.

I'd be inclined to call *Inner Running* a forgotten classic, except I can't tell that it was ever known well enough to have been forgotten. None of my runner friends has heard of it, let alone read it. It came into my possession only when my father came across an old mass-market edition in the back of a closet. (My father, not a runner but a student of all things inner, can't recall how he wound up with the book but is certain he never read it—the pristine condition of the spine before I got hold of it attests to this.)

But forgotten or never known, *Inner Running* deserves readers today more than ever. With every $250 Nike shoe guaranteed to make you run faster, with every FitBit or app that will quantify and analyze your every bodily movement, with every social media platform asking you to share the details of your run, the pressure for running to be objectified builds and we allow ourselves to be moved farther away from the simple fact and joy of being a body in motion.

Trail runners will recognize in themselves a natural affinity for Porter's approach. They are those—*we* are those—who surround ourselves with woods and rivers, with wild animals and cool shade, with desert air and sandy beaches while we play (and for the sake of all things holy, when we're doing it right it is *play*). Where better to appreciate beauty than running alone in nature? Where better to discover a meaningful life with a flourishing person at the center of experience?

And yet isn't trail running becoming more and more about miles and paces and races and elevations and who knows what? Aren't I crossing paths in the woods with more and more runners pushing buttons on gadgets and syncing up devices? More and more runners with phones plugged into their ears. Do they see the bird in the brush? Do they hear the wind through the trees? Do they feel the bliss of existence?

I say *they,* but of course I have myself in mind. It is only because I usually do not see the bird or hear the trees or find existence blissful that it's such a delight when I do. Porter's book is a reminder to these possibilities, a reminder that there are a multitude of ways of relating to our environments and that deliberate attention to one's inner experience while running is one possible way to live a good life.

We runners are lucky for many things. I now count *Inner Running* among these. You'll believe me when I tell you that on this morning's run I ran more slowly than usual, noticed to a new degree the variety of prairie grasses, felt happy and alive and eager for the coming gift of tomorrow's run.

If you are at all inclined toward the mystical, you too will resonate in such moments with Porter, when he writes, "You suddenly experience yourself doing the right thing at the right time for the right reasons; finally you're a round peg in a round hole. The universe is a vast cooperation. Everything's okay the way it is, because it is the way it is."

Runners, go out. And go in.

ON MY FEET

THE BLISTER ON MY RIGHT heel appears only after ten miles without socks in the red running shoes. But the divot in the callus of my left foot, that seems permanent. While the callus on my left pinky toe grows and recedes as I change from one pair of running shoes to another. My knee pain has vanished as my running shoes have gotten thinner and thinner, although the joints do crackle something structural when I get up in the morning. It's funny the red running shoes are the ones that blister my heel—the flimsy fabric of their heels has itself been ripped apart from use. The white running shoes are too big, and it must be said that wearing them in that marathon was a mistake. The green and yellow running shoes force me to wonder whether I'm quite fast enough to deserve them. Yet they lead me to thoughts of Oregon and Prefontaine, which is maybe why I wear them more than any other pair. The blue running shoes are clunky and I wear them only when my feet are tired and I want to go slow and watch the leaves fall or the ice thaw. When I have the energy, I run barefoot, or close to it, enjoying the feeling of the muscles of my feet flexing in the grass. My latest pair of running shoes had to double as painting shoes and are now caked in globs of white. Maybe they look artsy, hip, like they've been customized by someone with a pop-up boutique. Or maybe I just look a mess. Probably the latter. But twenty years, how many dozens of shoes, how many thousands of miles, and here I am still putting one foot in front of the other. Still on my feet, whatever's on my feet.

RUNNER ON THE ROAD!

MY SON LEARNED THE WORD *runner* this month. He's eighteen months old. We hike in the mountains every morning. Whenever we cross paths with a runner he takes the opportunity to shout "runner!" with absolute glee. Some runners are out of ear shot before he finds and delivers their label. Others will ignore him. But some will stop and say, "Yes, runner!" or offer a high-five.

When we don't see a runner for a while he will call out from his carrier on my back, "Daddy, run!" This is my cue to take off down the trail. He jostles and bounces and laughs, and when I stop he grants me a short break and then tells me to do it again. The whole month of August is passing us this way. And when I put him down on his own two feet, what do those feet do? Of course, they run. He bounds about and laughs, and when he falls down he gets back up.

It brings such joy to watch a child run, especially one who is just learning. Nietzsche said, "A man's maturity—consists in having found again the seriousness one had as a child, at play."

When I watch my son run, I take pleasure in his delight. I marvel at his discovery and celebration of his body. And I thank him for teaching me again how to run.

RUN AWAY

BAREST OF BONES, WHAT IS running? A way of moving from here to there. You've got your legs and your heart and your lungs and not much else to count on. You can cover a lot of ground this way. But there's one thing you can never get away from. No matter how far you run or how fast, you'll find yourself every time already there waiting for you when you stop.

Is this a cruelty or a form of enlightenment? After twenty years of experimentation, I'm inclined to answer this question, "Yes." As long as I keep trying to run away from myself I won't be able to. And as soon as I stop trying I won't need to.

There's no suitable resolution to these paradoxes except to drop them, to walk away, or, better, to run.

ON SOURDOUGH TRAIL,
MILES 3, 4.5, AND 9 (APPROX.)

THIS ESSAY'S ABOUT MOOSE. VERY simply that one summer I had three moose encounters on a particular trail in Montana. And how each time it was a bit scary but ultimately thrilling. And how seeing wild animals is wonderful and revelatory and humbling and primal and lots of other things but four adjectives in a series is already pushing it.

I ran that summer maybe a couple times a week on Sourdough Trail in the foothills of the Gallatin Mountains south of Bozeman. It's a wide trail that follows Sourdough Creek ten miles to its source at Mystic Lake. And it's one of the most popular trails in the area. Runners, hikers, mountain bikers, and their packs of excited dogs roam delightedly through the woods. I was preparing for a grueling mountain race and wanted to get in some long trail miles. Which is why I was spending so much time past the trail's three-mile mark. As crowded as the lower section of Sourdough is, the human presence falls precipitously after a few uphill miles. Above three, you'll see only the occasional other person.

Or moose. The first moose I saw on the trail was a little short of three miles at the trail's lone outhouse tucked away in the woods. I carry bear spray whenever I'm going to go much past Sourdough's four-mile mark. I put my hand on the spray in case I needed it against the moose, which in the open area we were in could easily have leveled me if so inclined. I ran by slowly and nervously with my head rotating to keep a line on the moose as it meandered into the woods perfectly indifferent to me.

A month later I was on my way back down the trail, some-where between miles five and four, a ways after crossing the trail's lone bridge, when I came around a bend and saw movement ahead of me on the trail, identified the cow moose and that it was moving away from me. I continued running; she continued moving away from me. When she moved off the trail I thanked her for letting me pass. "Gladly," she said. "Take pleasure in the texture of being," she said. There was nothing the least bit strange about this encounter.

Finally, soon after setting out for the return from Mystic Lake I met a bull on the trail. He invited me to play. I had no choice but to accept. He ran a quarter mile down the trail and waited. When I caught up with him he suggested another round. I obliged. We went on this way three or four rounds. And then there was silence in the woods and I felt alone. I wondered if the game were still ongoing and if he would ap-pear again ahead of me, but he did not appear again.

He had gone, and I had about nine miles left to run, and that was the last time I saw a moose on that trail, and I hope I see one again one day, and when people call Montana "the last best place" this is the kind of thing that makes them say it, and like I said above what a great thing it is to run with moose, and maybe it's not the safest situation in the world but at least it wasn't an angry bear, and what ever would we have different anyway? Would we refrain from woods? Would we begrudge the moose who reside there? Of course not. This is a happy essay.

OLD MAN IN THE PARK

You got yourself a real goer there. On his way
to a marathon, by the looks of it. How old is he?
Two? Boy, you're gonna wear your daddy out.
    Keep it up, too.   He don't mind a bit.

The old man in the park is right. I don't mind.
And how that word *goer* falls like rain on my ear.
I savor it, pausing to wonder how soon I'll find
reason to make that sweet sound myself, even

as my boy is already gone down the trail.

ON THE USES OF THINGS LIKE BODIES

I SHOW UP TO TRACK practice at age thirty-eight having been to very few track practices in my life and not entirely convinced that track practice is a good idea. After all, track practice isn't much fun. You run harder than you'd like to, you put yourself in pain, you make yourself feel sick, and worst of all there's no compelling reason for you to be doing any of this. You just are. And having only yourself to blame compounds the futility of the effort.

By definition things that seem fun are fun and things that don't, aren't.

Except, we're running 1,000m repeats with one-minute rests between and it is hard and it is painful and I feel sick in the last 300m of each 1,000 trying to keep up with Sophia, who is young and fast and pacing me and encouraging me, and for some reason I'm enjoying all of this.

I'm not training for anything in particular. My goals are undefined. Again, there's no particular reason for me to be doing this. And yet. There's undeniable satisfaction to hard work, there's pleasure within freely chosen pain. The sickness will pass.

And closer to home, there is the relief of the rests, the camaraderie of mutual *Good job*s with Sophia, the loose gooey feeling in my legs that will still be with me tomorrow, the fact that I already feel more powerful than I was before the workout, and the very rightness of a thing put to its proper use. What good is a book that isn't read? A car that isn't driven? A body that isn't run hard?

Within the limits of what my body is capable today I celebrate myself pushing myself in these repeating 1,000s on a summer's night alive and happy.

Until the sixth repeat when Sophia finally drops me.

But please do not read any sentiment in my fading back at the end of this essay, for I am still breathing hard, still doing what I can, and when I finish this 1,000 and rest arms akimbo I assure you it will be with satisfaction.

ON WHAT DOES AND DOES NOT FEEL GOOD:
A DISCOVERY

THE SECOND WEDNESDAY OF EACH month unless the month is January or February (or in my case, because it was snowing that day too, March) runners in my town huddle in front of a different brewery and await the start of one of the more charmingly underformalized, undertechnologized, undermeasured , and underseriousled races anyone's likely to show up for these days.

The race is scheduled for six, but month after month the race director delays to wait for stragglers. We start at 6:05 or 6:10 or . . . I don't really know. I don't wear a watch, so I'm just guessing. Kind of like how the person who measures the course guesses what 5K means (3ish miles, generally). It's fine that the distance is approximate. There is a race clock (most times) but no one tracks individual times or even finishing order. The only reason you get a bib when you register is to enter a raffle and to get a free beer after the finish. That's about it for context: you run 3ish miles in 20ish or 30ish or 40ish minutes, and then you have a beer, and it's all very charming in a small-town Montana kind of way.

This month we ran at Madison River Brewing in Belgrade. One thing about running races in Montana is runners are shy about taking the starting line. It's a strange cultural habit for newcomers and visitors to behold. No other community I've encountered has a similar practice or, no matter how open-minded and liberal, could begin to imagine the merits of such conduct. Anyway, I can't see the merits. So I toe the starting line—alone or almost—knowing full well that some number of the runners lingering behind will pass me. This month there were six of them. Make that five. One of the runners who beat me, credit to him, also started at the start line. I knew I was running seventh because I could count the runners as they passed me, but my place was confirmed by a spectator standing about three blocks from the finish saying, "Nice job, seventh," to me and "nice job, eighth," to the guy behind me. A note about this eighth: The courses for these races are, I emphasize, informal. You look for the small cones on the ground and do your best to stay in line with them. Last summer I was part of a small pack who missed a cone and ran three blocks in the wrong direction before figuring it out at the Katabatic race. Anyway, there are honest mistakes and close-enoughs. But this eighth guy. I knew he was close enough for me to have heard his number called out by the spectator, but I couldn't sense him as being close enough to threaten passing me. I followed the yellow-green cones to the end of the block and turned right to make it kitty-corner to the finish in Lewis and Clark Park only to see Eighth Guy and his accomplice, Ninth Guy, come barreling on a tangent to try to clip me at the finish. You'll understand, I hope, that despite the informality of the race, despite the lack of individual times, despite everything I say about running being its own reward, despite resting comfortably on my they're-only-cheating-themselves laurels, my feeling was *Fuck those guys*. They didn't clip me at the finish. And I hope by some happenstance they're reading this now and learning the ignominy of not only getting beat or even of getting beat while cheating but of then being called out for it in this forum. This is for you, Eighth Guy and Ninth Guy. Heart of hearts, you know who you are.

There.

Do I feel better having written that?

Not really.

But I'll tell you when I did feel better. I felt better when I ran as well as I could have hoped that day. I felt better when I saw my wife holding our son along the racecourse and he yelled "Yay, Daddy!" I felt so good when I heard that. And I feel so good now just writing that. It comes right back. And the beer at the brewery that was good too, But not as good as my son feeling proud of me. That's something else entirely.

ON FAILURE

To be merely very good in a world
That recognizes only the truly great
Is to have made sacrifices
To an indifferent God

But if God is absolute
Failure remains relative
And best cousin to good

To run is to run
Is to run is to run

Or can be

TODAY'S RUN

THERE'S NOT MUCH BETTER THAN running in a gentle rain. When I set out this morning I had those passing thoughts, *I hope I don't get too cold* and *Despite what I tell myself, isn't running in the sun pretty alright* and *Aren't I due for a day off anyway.* Luckily, I've been running long enough to not always listen to my thoughts. Let them do their thing, I've learned to say, I'll do mine. Onto the trail. I was cold enough to regret not wearing gloves, but only at the start. After I few minutes I was warm enough to uncover my hands from my sleeves and pull off my hood. I remembered a sentence from a Denis Johnson story: "I knew every raindrop by its name." That's how I felt. Each drop was like a kiss on my forehead. I don't mean to be so poetic about it. But that is how it felt. There I was huffing and puffing and slipping in the mud while the rain kissed my forehead among the trees. Mud like mortar holding the bricks of my shoes to the ground, I was hardly running, which was fine by me. I'd be out there longer. And when I came to the creek I stopped. The water ran slowly, a small stick floated over to the bank. I watched and listened to the birds and felt the rain and it felt good and I felt good and I could have started to run again but chose instead to linger and try to let my thoughts be like water and let nature soothe me until I was like nature or until I was nature, and maybe I was nature the whole time—who can say what is nature?—so I made a mental photograph of the creek and the small log that lay part way across just upstream and I made the photograph black and white and I sharpened the contrast on the log and the grass as far as I could stretch my imagination but the water stayed soft as the rain was gentle through my field of vision and on my legs and on my face. I could have lingered longer but I started to run again, still feeling good, still feeling embraced by my environment. Back at the car I cleaned off in a puddle, then I drove to a cafe, ordered coffee, and sat down with this pen in my hand.

MEDITATION

MY LEGS ARE SORE TODAY and I'm taking stock of things. My job frustrates me. My small town frustrates me. The decisions that have brought my family to live here are the source of not insignificant regret for me. I am unsure of my purpose and prospects as a writer. I feel tired and burned out. I am accepting for the first time that I am not unfamiliar with stress, which I have always imagined to be beneath me. Worst of all, I notice resentment creeping into me at my having to adapt to the contours of the world and my place in it. All of this is complete nonsense. But knowing it doesn't always relieve it.

My legs are sore today, and when I walk gingerly to the counter to ask the barista for a refill this brings me a true and simple pleasure. My body feels well used without feeling overused and it is hard to maintain self-pity in this condition. Each careful step reminds me of how my muscles have been used and how they will be used.

My mind turns to this afternoon's run. Will I run this route or that one? Will I wear these shoes or those? Already I feel the gloom taking its leave of me. I know myself well enough to know this leave will be temporary, but I know too that there will be another run to follow today's and with luck another and another for decades to come.

I do not believe that through running I am merely forestalling an inevitable reckoning with myself. Rather, I think that in running I am doing the very things I must aspire to in the rest of my life: being myself, accepting my limitations, adapting to present circumstances, engaging fully with the world, and enjoying the true and simple pleasure of existence.

The day I wake without another run to look forward to will be the day I find out how much I've learned from running about how to live the rest of my life.

OF MARATHON

Athens ahead: an abecedary
beginning before its beginning,
committing, claiming, closing
distance from alpha to omega.
Easy it is to entertain entreaties
from friendly footfalls foreseen
given how grace & greatness
hide. How hurried and hurt he
is inside the illuminated I——
Jogging? You must be joking.
Keep kicking, keep keeping on
like legs long on leisure last.
Midway on marathon morning,
no one nowhere has nothing
on our odds—over & onward.
Promise please these prayers:
Quit quit quit, but not quite yet.
Run the race a mile at a time, a
series of strides—& stay still——
time and terminus converging.

Until uh-oh you undergo your undoing under unprecedented & unanticipated & unavoidable vicissitudes ventured into via viva vivo vivere va-va-va-vrooooom. Voluntarily violated: voila! Wait wait wait! Withstand? Withdraw? What difference? We wonder what will we will. What x-factor exactly extends excruciating exertion from extreme exercise to existential exorcism? You yourself your legs your body—yuck!—your mind—yuck!—your soul, in every way you, by Zeus by Zeno by zip by zoom, zapped with zilch to go. Zero-point-zero yet zero remains from the final point-two.

RUN FREE

A WISE MAN ONCE SAID, "When you write, then you remember." I'm taking his advice and writing down some of the other wise things he has said.

Mental fitness plays a big role during competition. If you don't rule your mind, your mind will rule you. That's the way I think about this sport.

Only the disciplined ones are free in life. If you are undisciplined, you are a slave to your moods. You are a slave to your passions.

To win is not important. To be successful is not even important. How to plan and prepare is crucial. When you plan very well and prepare very well, then success can come on the way. Then winning can come on your way.

Pleasure in what you are doing is what puts perfection in your work—that's a quote by Aristotle.

I always tell people that this is a really simple deal: Work hard. If you work hard, follow what's required and set your priorities right, then you can really perform without taking shortcuts. If you're taking shortcuts, you can't be free.

Become comfortable with being uncomfortable. Accept change.

When I run, I feel good. My mind feels good. I sleep in a free way, and I enjoy life.

No human is limited.

The mind is what drives a human being. If you have that belief—pure belief in your heart—that you want to be successful then you can talk to your mind and your mind will control you to be successful.

My mind is always free. My mind is flexible. That is why I wear this band on my wrist.

I want to show the world that you can go beyond your thoughts, you can break more than you think you can break.

I enjoy the simplistic training and life in marathon. You run, eat, sleep, walk around—that's how life is. You don't get complicated. The moment you get complicated it distracts your mind.

Living simply sets you free.

Now that I've written these down, allow me a moment to let them sink in.

How long did you give me?

I fear it wasn't enough.

If Eliud Kipchoge were here right now, this is what I'd like to ask him: If writing leads to remembering, does remembering something make it part of you? If you make something part of yourself, does it change who you are? If I am always changing, how do I become myself? Is it really possible for anyone to develop a grace like yours? How, one more time, are we to be free?

My dream is to make this world a running world. A running world is a healthy world. A running world is a wealthy world. A running world is a peaceful world. A running world is a joyful world.

There is freedom in running. Go and run and your mind will be free. That is what is needed in the whole planet.

DISPATCHES FROM THE WILD ROGUE RELAY

MARCH 31, 2013. DURING ONE leg of the 2008 Cascade Lakes Relay Jim Brendle was running alone on a remote stretch of highway amidst the ambient glow of almost-dawn. A large owl glided out over his head and hung there a moment before disappearing back into the woods. It was a brief moment, but it was the kind of experience that can deeply affect a person. For Brendle, it was the inspiration to start the Smoky Mountain Relay in North Carolina in 2010 with the support of the Douglass family, organizers of CLR. And in June, five summers after seeing that owl, Brendle will inaugurate the Wild Rogue Relay, a 200-plus-mile race in southern Oregon.

Brendle has been devoted to relay races since first encountering the atmosphere and camaraderie of Hood to Coast in 2006. His enthusiasm has only grown in the meantime, and he's confident that Wild Rogue will prove the most beautiful of all the relays. The course wends from Applegate Lake near the California border north then west along the Rogue River to Gold Beach, with three of the race's final four legs on the beach. The route is intentionally secluded—much of it is inaccessible to car—and this, Brendle believes, will reward the runners, who will witness uncommon natural beauty throughout the race.

There will be artificial attractions as well, including music along the racecourse, a Dutch Bros midnight coffee party in the forest, and (fire permits pending) s'mores. Money raised from the race will go to support Jackson County Special Olympics. This first year the race will be capped at seventy teams, leaving at the time of this writing about half the spots still available, but one of them already assigned to your correspondent's Big Cats.

Race Weekend, June 21 – 22, 2013. Coach Katie was at the end of her substantial organizational wits trying to coordinate rides and flights to Medford for a team of runners hailing from Portland, Seattle, D. C., Minneapolis, and (thanks to a race-saving last-minute substitution for an injured runner) Ashland. The whole thing involved two whiteboards full of contingency plans and dozens of frantic emails, phone calls, and forum posts. One of the first things you learn running a relay race is they are often logistical spider webs in which you and your teammates are both the spider and the fly. In an admirable attempt to relieve some of the stress, Coach's brother (your diligent correspondent) and several teammates pursued a strategy of levity cum immaturity that Coach officially "did not appreciate." However, let the record show that on the eve of the race Coach was briefly sighted hucking water balloons in the parking lot of the Medford Best Western.

It turns out the racecourse for the Wild Rogue Relay runs 213 miles from Applegate Lake, a short walk from the world's only Bigfoot trap, to the mouth of the Rogue in Gold Beach. It requires two vans of six runners each (unless you're insane, which a great many of the participants seemed to be, in which case six runners and one van) who will run round the clock through forests, over mountains, along rivers, deep into the realm of pain.

Friday morning our team's Van 1 drove down to the start-line to check in while Van 2 headed for the Medford airport to pick up two runners arriving that morning. At check-in we were given a list of emergency satellite numbers, which we were quickly advised did not work. We were similarly advised that if one of our runners had a heart attack outside of cell phone coverage we should strongly consider getting some coverage. There was some disagreement among Van 1 whether the lack of support was a bug in the event or one of its most appealing features (correct answer: the latter). Regardless, we hoped for the best and put our first runner to the line. Van 2 arrived moments ahead of the start and for the first time Big Cats was united.

Assuming a full squad, each runner runs three times, three to nine miles a go. If dehydration, facial expression, and sunburn are any indication, the central challenge of the first set of legs was solar. The temperature wasn't much above eighty, but with a little elevation, direct sunlight, and miles of road, that's more than sufficient to unsettle even a strongly constituted runner.

One of the things you learn to appreciate in a relay race is the sanctity of a good bowel movement, the failure of which to achieve invariably becomes the source of much digestion-themed humor. Unfortunately for you (or not), much of this material is unsuitable for a family newspaper, and we'll have to leave the subject with one Big Cat who boasted that his GI tract alone could provide at least two column inches of anecdote.

With first legs complete, Van 1 recouped from the heat at Red Lily Vineyards, sampling wine, cooling off in the Applegate River, and receiving massages from Therapeutic Associates. Some tantalizing consideration here of scrapping the race and spending the weekend right there, but no.

Near dusk we moved into a section of the race along the Rogue River and watched the moon come up fat over the mountains. It glowed generously enough above us that as night fell several of our runners elected to turn their headlamps off and run by the natural light. The timing of the race did preclude what I imagine were some magnificent views, although for the acrophobes among us the darkness did also hide the vertigo-inducing canyon drops. At the race's midpoint, along a BLM road up in the Klamath Mountains, Dutch Bros. Coffee was serving up breve lattes at the second of their three free stands along the course.

It wasn't all good at night, though. While it's possible that your reporter offered a day's small fame in exchange for printable antics, that's not why one Big Cat, barreling down a mountain at 3 a.m., took a bad step in a pothole-filled gravel road and tumbled Asics over clavicles to a bloody stop at the bottom of a drainage ditch, his ankle already rising like the blueberry muffin it still is at the time of this publication as he got up to run six more miles to meet his van.

After driving ahead while Van 2 took their second legs, Van 1 found a patch of grass where we could spread out a tarp and lie down, despite the breves, zonked. With the entire course running through mountains, forests, and farms, it's a rare hour that at least one person doesn't say, "this is so beautiful," but the view we woke up to in the Klamaths after two hours of sleep was positively sublime. A dense white fog flowed wet and heavy between either side of the evergreen gorge below us, yet the air stayed dry and crisp up where we were, witnessing it all light softly up.

By the time you reach the third set of legs you're kind of just hanging on. You're tired, you're sore, but the end is in sight. If you've successfully spent the past twenty-four hours getting in and out of a cramped stinky van between runs, you'll be able to finish your third run no matter just about anything. However, do pity those runners who thought a beach run would be fun under such conditions. One of the Wild Rogue Relay's selling points is that three of the final four legs are on the sand. Buyer beware and know well your private sense of "fun."

Big Cats crossed the finish line mid-afternoon and swiftly convened at the after-party, where Ashland's Standing Stone Brewing Co. was serving one free pint per runner. Their Twin Plunge Double IPA now comes to you reportorially recommended. As we swapped stories and compared sorenesses between our two vans we generated an impressive registry of wildlife: We had seen several deer and a few lizards, interrupted a cow and a bull *in delicto*, nearly run over a wild turkey, had one runner claim somewhat credibly to have smelled a bear during her night run, seen a beach layered in sea lions, heard a confirmed account of multiple great white sharks just off the coast, and encountered a strange specimen of indeterminate entomological classification with an elongated thorax smashed to our windshield. No sign of bigfoot.

We also confirmed our suspicion that Dane Train, a team of young runners who blew by us near the start of the race looking archetypally suited to the task, won the race—by nearly three hours.

Around Gold Beach that evening and the following morning, residents must have wondered at the packs of athletic-looking strangers limping around in sweatpants. To any of them reading this: I won't begin to try to make us make sense, but I will say, Hope to see you next year!

HOW TO LOSE A TOENAIL IN STYLE

ON THE THURSDAY BEFORE HOOD to Coast in 2005 I got a phone call from our Leg I runner, who was dropping out with some lame excuse or another. We had one day till the race and no one to run down the hill from Timberline.

I called my sister and said, "Hey, Coach, who can we get on such short notice?"

She went through her network of Portland runners, but everyone by then was either already on a team or had to work.

Resigned to making do with eleven runners, we started packing our bags and thinking about a pasta dinner. Then Joe called. Joe Bear, my college roommate, who had run Hood to Coast with us a few years before. He was in Portland for the night and on his way to Produce Row.

By the time I met him there, hours had passed, enough for a few beers at least. Would the alcohol work for me or against me? I hugged Joe, declined a cigarette, and hit him straight off with, "What do you think about getting up in the morning, driving to Mt. Hood, and running six miles straight downhill?"

His eyes steadied on me as he considered his response. A strange sequence of ruminative grunts emerged from somewhere behind his sternum. Suddenly, he banged his fist on the table and shouted, "I'm in! Now buy me a beer."

Joe told me to pick him up early in the morning. As he approached the car I looked out the window and took in the tall, unshaven, and presumably hungover man in jeans and

73

cowboy boots. "There's our runner!"

Seated next to me, squinting over his aviators, Joe said, "First stop, Goodwill."

Why Goodwill? That would be for the running clothes: a Team USA #25 singlet from the eighties, it turned out, and almost-matching shorts no bigger than underwear.

"Next stop, shoe store."

It is generally considered unwise to race down steep mountains in brand-new shoes, but if your other option is cowboy boots what are you gonna do?

What to make of Joe at the start line? What did the other runners think of this strangely dressed man—his thin, hairy body barely covered, his tube socks, his large dark glasses? It's possible few expected it when Joe blazed down the mountain first in his wave of runners—his long, gangly stride accentuating his rail shape.

But those of us who knew Joe weren't surprised by his performance. Nor were we surprised when, after the exchange, he removed a shoe to reveal a blood-soaked sock and, underneath that, a big toe sans nail.

Nothing a can of Oly wouldn't fix.

RUNNING WITH THE STARS

IT WAS ALREADY ONE OF those runs that remind me why I run.

Hood to Coast leg 20, five and three-quarter miles consisting of two significant climbs on the gravel and dust of Pittsburgh Road somewhere in those uncanny middle-of-the-night miles between St. Helens and Mist. The night sky was scattershot with stars, and I would gladly have run uphill till sunrise.

I like to think that I run for myself—for the physical joy of moving my body through space, for the mental and emotional serenity that results from physical exertion, for the way running amplifies my sense of being a living, breathing, sweating creature who belongs to this planet—but I know I sometimes run for other runners too. Namely, the ones I'm passing.

In the darkness, the runners ahead of me appeared as stars, points of bouncing white light in the black. My roadkill amassed as quickly as I could count them. I was running so easily it was as if I were flying through the night, reaching one star and allowing my momentum to shoot me off for the next.

So enraptured was I that I didn't notice the single point of light approaching me faster than I could escape it until I heard its carrier breathing and kicking up rocks. This guy was moving.

I reminded myself of all the profound reasons for which I ran and maturely cautioned myself against competition. So what if I got passed? No shame in that. So what if I was only the second fastest runner for the stretch of the race? And yet, inevitably, my legs ignored their instructions. As we crested the second hill with a little less than a mile to run I found myself in full chase.

I narrowed the gap but only to spur the other runner faster along. He denied my attempt to pass and forced me to settle in behind him. For the remainder of the leg I would not be able to regain the lead and he would not be able to drop me, and pretty soon we would cease trying. We ran—*I* ran—on the very edge of abandon (and probably over it). We covered dips and maneuvered curves like we had grown up on this road—lucky because we were running it basically blind, outrunning the beams of our headlamps. I came to feel that we were bound up, like our stars had fallen into mutual orbit and that either without the other would lose course and vanish into the night.

And suddenly it was over. We handed off our bracelets and bent, hands on knees, gasping for air. After a moment of recovery we embraced and he showed me a number on his watch—our mile pace over the final descent—that was smaller than any I'd ever been associated with before. Immediately, I latched onto that number, sharing it with my teammates in the van, and savoring the warm swell of pride in my chest.

But when I think of that run now the number eludes me and so does the pride. What returns is the sense of moving so freely among the stars.

AN ORAL HISTORY OF JOE PARKER,
SELF-DESCRIBED HOOD TO COAST LEGEND,
BY THOSE WHO KNOW HIM WELL

You'll hear my name echoing on most every leg along the route.
—Joe

(Mary, sister) True, Joe ran cross-country at Grant [High School, Portland]. Then when Ralph and I were living in Eugene and Joe was a student he'd run over to our house, but that might have had as much to do with drinking beer and watching the Ducks with Ralph as it did with running.

(Martha, sister) Big Bad Joe. I think the thing he loved about running was leaving his sweaty shirts and socks around for Mary and me to pick up. If that gives you some indication.

(Sally, wife) Joe ran Hood to Coast more than a dozen times in the eighties and nineties, for a while on a team called the Lemmings. I remember one year his team estimated its time badly and at the end of the race was the only team left on the course. When they finally came in the beach party was shut down. All that was left was a half-deflated two-story Spuds McKenzie flapping sadly in the wind.

(Brian, nephew) Growing up, we were always hearing Joe talk about Hood to Coast, so eventually we decided to put together a family team. Except Joe ended up being injured and couldn't run with the team. So he drove the second van and was basically in extreme team-manager mode the whole time.

(Scott, nephew) We were kind of a random bunch. Katie just quit one day, deciding she hated running. Jerry kept trying to convince us to ditch the van and ride five bicycles alongside our runner. Brian claimed at one point, speciously, I think, that he'd never run more than three consecutives miles. In any case, we weren't what you'd call experienced.

(Katie, niece) Yeah, okay, I quit that year. But to this day I'm the only one organized enough to fill Joe's shoes as a team manager—as evinced by the year we put Scott in charge.

(Scott) There is such a thing as over preparation.

(Gina, niece) He really did line us up in his kitchen before the race to practice handoffs. Now, keep in mind the caliber of runner here. We would pace as a team like ten-minute miles.

(Sara, friend of Gina's) And then there's the clipboard. Gina was a mess about the whole clipboard thing.

(Gina) Even now I can't see a clipboard without breaking into a sweat. Someone in our van wasn't recording the times. And Joe had made such a big deal about the importance— no, it was more like the *sanctity*—of the clipboard. Whatever happened on the course, the clipboard was not to be compromised. I really thought Joe might throw me off the team when we got to the next van exchange and he found out what happened. I asked Sally what to do and she said to just make up the times, Joe would never know.

(Katie) From Timberline to Seaside you have to be Total Race Face all the way. I learned that from Joe.

(Scott) And then didn't he do some weird thing where he tried to convince one of our runners she was injured and that only he could sub in for her and then run across the finish line?

(Sally) We were at one of the van exchanges and he had his running clothes on. I remember saying to him, "Honestly, you're so eager to run a leg it sounds like you're hoping someone gets hurt."

(Brian) He laced up his shoes and jumped in the race. Except our runner wasn't even injured, so she just kept running and they ended up running side by side.

(Sally) Gina and Sara played this song—

(Gina and Sara) *I'll see you when you get there, If you ever get there!*

(Sally) And we all learned it and were singing along with the windows down. Then we saw Joe standing on the sidewalk with his clipboard just shaking his head at us. It was nineteen years till there was another family team.

NOT EVEN TO THE RIVER YET

where I run to undo the burdens
of this complicated life
                                    —bisecting my line
a buck, three, four small points,
bounding down the avenue en
route for return.

Strangely, I see, we're in this together
as he turns east and parallels me,
misshaped shadow to my misshaped man.
Mississippi bound, we
sense there is sense there, shadows
in search of a tangible sustaining.

A dog barks.
The buck breaks
down an alley.
I stop. Humans
appear on the scene
with cameras.

There is nothing more to see, but

the river
          the river
                    the river
is there
                    yet.

WHY RUN?

WHY DO WE RUN? WHAT do we get out of it? Or, perhaps more accurately, what do we hope to get out of it?

It's tautologically clear that it would be easier not to run. Even those of us for whom running is one of the great sources of joy in our lives have to admit it is effort. Never mind the particulars: the hassles of changing clothes and planning routes, the struggling up hills, the sweating, the chafing, and so on. We don't even have to go anywhere. We could literally just stay right where we are.

But we don't. We go. And we do so in a society that is both over-worked and impatient in its demand for gratification. Running is therefore anathema to an American Good Time. It's voluntary work, and the gratifications it brings are decidedly eventual. What I want to submit is that runners are runners in large part because they have confirmed what if you're lucky someone told you when you were young: that most things in life worth having take sacrifice and commitment. Running's rewards are of this kind. The more you do it, the better you get at it, the more joy it *can* bring you.

The *can* in the previous sentence is in italics: that's the crux here. Because on the flip side of being fitter and faster, more comfortable in your body, and more at home in the physical world is overdoing it, turning running into an obligation, a chore. It is possible to suck the fun right out of it.

So to the questions *Why do we run? What do we get out of it? Or, what do we hope to get out of it?* I'd like to add one more: How do we push ourselves without pushing too far?

The very mention of pushing oneself will bring Steve

Prefontaine to many runners' minds. He better than anyone embodied the gutsy and swaggering attitude of the runner. He articulated it better than anyone else too: "Somebody may beat me, but they are going to have to bleed to do it."

That idea of refusing to be outworked can become a cliché. How easy it is to recall the video montages extolling impossible workouts and stoic self-sacrifice. (You've noticed the heroes of these videos never have time for watching TV themselves.) But for something to become a cliché it must contain truth. The kinds of athletes who get asked about the intensity of their training are usually those who have achieved a great deal in their sport. And part of having done so is having worked extremely hard.

Take Heather Kampf. Kampf, an NCAA champion at 800m who placed seventh in the 2012 Olympic Trials at the same distance, has this to say about pushing herself: "There's always another gear. Your body will send signals to slow down because, physiologically, it doesn't like going as hard as you are. But you can override those signals to some degree. I always tell myself I can push through. There's always more to discover. I like to put myself on the edge and find out what I'm made of."

The really interesting word in there is *discover*. It's true, we don't know anything about our limits until we've broken them. You can't run a six-minute mile until, suddenly, you do. And then, maybe 5:50 is within reach. Maybe 5:30. How fast can you go? But there are limits to pushing limits. And you can only see them in retrospect. Push yourself enough and eventually you will discover it was too much—too far, too fast, too often, too *something*. You only get to run your best once, and for a long time you don't have the privilege of knowing if you already have.

A friend of mine, when he was fourteen, was one of the best marathoners in the country for his age. But his life moved in other directions and he quit running for over twenty years. When he returned he built himself back up and after a couple years was able to improve on his previous times and again become competitive in his age group. He won some races, travelled the globe for big international marathons, and decided to step up his training to try for a PR in Chicago. What happened? An injury, fairly serious. Then another one. Now he's rehabbing again, hoping to get back out there and give it another shot.

For some runners, that's the game. You have to be willing to go too far if you want to find out how far you can go. You have to be willing to put in the miles, put in the hours, forgo this indulgence or that one (realistically, you have to forgo this indulgence *and* that one). You have to find the willpower to get yourself out of bed those mornings when it's raining and you're tired and still sore from yesterday, the determination to keep going those afternoons when it's hot and you're about to puke and you have ten more repeats to do and you can't for the life of you remember why you do this. You have to be willing to suffer, to really suffer—physical and mental anguish—for the sake of achievement and the meaning that attends.

The harder you work, the greater the reward: that's the orthodox view of running. A less orthodox view might raise the question of whether there's an upper limit of where the rewards correspond to the increased effort. Maybe if I trained more I could be faster, but maybe being faster doesn't mean as much to me as it does to enjoy the runs that get me there. What if we aren't like Heather Kampf and we don't have to be? What if my friend didn't have to set a new PR? What if I were freed from the pressure to accomplish something in my running? What if the reason we get out of bed on those rainy mornings when we're tired and we've got a full day of work ahead of us isn't because we have to but because we want to? What if the work of running is the reward itself? What if running—just you, out there, in your body, in your environment, in whatever mental state you're in, moving, discovering, playing—what if this is the joy? What then?

FAIR-WEATHERED RUNNER

ONE THING ABOUT GROWING UP running in western Oregon is not ever learning how to run in the cold or the snow (or even appreciating that cold and snow are actually distinct running conditions). Many Oregonians go on to discover warm clothes, layers, spikes, etc., and make do in the Midwest or the Rocky Mountains. I've been a decade in these locals (six years in Minnesota, four in Montana) and I still don't know how to run in more than shorts, shoes, usually a shirt, and on sunny days a visor. Basically I've spent my last ten Decembers – Aprils (give or take) watching the NBA and putting on what my wife affectionately calls my "winter weight." When the melt comes I'm stir-crazy and eager to get out and get some miles in. The legs always can remember what to do, even if they're not very good at it the first week or two. The fitness comes back more slowly each year. The speed, such as it was, is like a friend from my youth who I've lost touch with. Regardless, the summers and falls are ideal for running, and I enjoy the hell out of running almost every day.* But as good as half the year has been to me in these places, there's something I still miss from the good old Willamette Valley: the rain. What are rest months for me now used to be rain months, used to be soaking wet afternoons before 4:30 sunset, used to be mist or drizzle or spring showers. Used to be the secret appointments I kept with myself. Used to be a

---

* Slight amendment here: fire season in Montana is a major disruption to what I'm otherwise calling "ideal," and let's not forget those Midwest days that are ninety-plus degrees and sweatier than a gym sock.

dimension of reality only I had access to. When it rains in Montana now, as when it rained in Minnesota while I lived there, I know it's warm out and I should take advantage of the occasion. Usually I do. And while I treasure these sometimes rain runs I miss their regular presence in my life the way you might miss your cousin Gina if she moved to France and you got to see her only over the holidays, which would be better than not seeing her at all and would make your time with her more precious but would not ever make you stop wishing you could see her all the time and that your kids could grow up together in the rain the way the two of you did.

RACE READY

I just want to come out and give it my best;
I've put in the work and today is just about enjoying that;
It'll take a big effort and a few things going my way;
You never know in a race like this; anything could happen;
I'm ready; I'm relaxed; I feel good;
You have to trust the race plan and run smart, trust the
        process;
My workouts have been phenomenal and my coach says
        I'm ready,
I just have to run my race;
It's going to come down to who gets across the line first;
I think the fastest runner will win;
It's in God's hands now;
Wish me luck!

MEET ME IN EUGENE
A TRACK AND FIELD REPORT

Olympic Trials, Day 1

BEING AT A WORLD-CLASS TRACK and field meet is nothing like watching one on TV. If you've ever cussed at your screen when the network cuts to commercial in the middle of a 5,000m race you understand the fact of editorial control, but until you've been at a major meet you can't appreciate the degree. What being at a world-class track and field meet is like is being at a high school track and field meet with better athletes. There are at least three events to follow at all times, plus athletes taking victory laps for events just finished and athletes warming up for events soon to come. Not to mention, you might not even be in the stadium just now but out in the pavilion grabbing a beer or watching your kid run sprint races on the turf field. And every once in a while, in whatever part of the hoopla you find yourself, you might notice your eyes drifting up toward the sky-blue sky and the evergreens gently rocking in the lazy summer breeze on the hill above you and, reportorial duties be damned, letting your thoughts go slack, thinking in the privacy of own mind no particular thing at all.

Maybe that last part was just me. I arrived in Eugene for the Olympic Trials in more of a recreational than professional capacity. I had a press pass, which I planned to use more for its perks than for its responsibilities. Ahead of me lay four days of leisure and intermittent nostalgia for my undergraduate days. Of course, the University of Oregon I attended a decade-plus ago bore only a family resemblance to the University of Nike I found in its place. On my way to pick up my pass at a building that I didn't know existed, next to a basketball stadium I didn't know could be imagined, I passed a moated building and briefly—but only briefly—entertained a what-if scenario wherein I majored in business rather than philosophy.

After flying in to Portland and driving down to Eugene with my sister, Katie, that morning and getting credentialed, the fresh punch of an IPA was just what the moment required. Outside Hayward Field, on closed-off Agate Street, I bought my first Ninkasi Beer Run of the trials and elbowed Katie excitedly to indicate Bob Kersee standing nearby.

My plan was to enjoy the beer and the sunshine and let the day come at me as it would. That lasted until I heard Jeremy Wariner's name called over the loudspeaker and rushed into the stadium flashing my press pass like it was my job. Warnier, the old veteran, twelve years removed from his Olympic gold in the event, qualified for the semifinals in the 400m on time. After the race, I caught him in the media tent, where he spoke in warm and generous clichés about setting an example for the younger runners and helping them to surpass himself. Easy dude to root for, I concluded.

Back in the stadium for the women's 400m, I climbed up to the sparsely peopled media tribune at the top of the grandstand and spread out under the overhang. It would be possible to spend an entire Eugene summer enjoying the back and forth between sunshine and shade.

The fans in Tracktown are just as smart and dialed in as everyone says they are. They will cheer so loudly for an obscure field result that they delay the start of races on the track. It's great. That first evening, when the heats for the women's 400m got underway, it was shocking to see in person just how much the runners faded down the homestretch. The whole race is about who can forestall collapse the longest. Only Allyson Felix ran the whole thing consistently, the announcer calling attention to her "so so smooth stride." While it's true her stride is as smooth as Steph Curry's jump shot, it felt a little at odds with the spirit of camaraderie to single her out mid-race, not to mention a little pervy in tone.

The only previous time I had seen Galen Rupp run in person was in 2004 when he tried to achieve a four-minute mile as a high schooler. I've followed his career, though, since high school, when I missed racing against him in cross-country by one year. The allegations of his cheating under the raging influence of Alberto Salazar are substantial at this point, but I can't bring myself to watch his races with anything but cautious optimism.

For Day 1's culminating race at Hayward, the 10,000m runners took a handful of 100m strides up and down the homestretch and after quick introductions were sent off to do their best. Anyone who tells you distance races in track are boring is telling you more about themselves than about racing. There's as much drama and tension as any viewer has the capacity to appreciate. Rupp started the race in second and stayed there for about six laps before zooming way out ahead of the field. On the eighth lap, in a scene out of a Prefontaine movie, he looked over his shoulder to see just how far ahead he was. Here he let his lead evaporate, and I got the strong sense that he was toying with the other runners. Either he was running the race as a workout or trying to break other runners with his changes of speed. After twelve laps he surged again. This time a few runners tried to stay with him. One by one he dropped them—in Bernard Lagat's case, dramatically—and ran on to an easy win.

Day 2

The morning of the women's 10,000m I showed up early to stake out a spot on the landing directly above the start and finish of the race. The runners lined up close enough that they looked for once like actual muscle-and-bone people. I could see whose body language betrayed nerves, who couldn't believe she was really there, and what kind of shoes they all wore. It was among the best spots in Hayward, and I lasted about half the race there before an official told me it was for coaches only and I had to hike up to the media tribune.

In the field, long jumpers warmed up, barely touching the runway as they glided toward the pit, and discusses sailed placid arcs through the sky. It was a tranquil scene interrupted gracefully then violently by a wayward discuss that nearly hit one of the jumpers before rolling out onto the track. The jumper was understandably shook, and luckily all the runners were on the far side of the track, the race not yet as spread as it would be.

Molly Huddle led from the start and was extending her lead lap by lap over the field. Pretty soon she was lapping runners and forcing upon me one of the most pressing questions of the meet: Why do some lapped runners not give up the inside lane? None of the possible answers is encouraging. At best, runners are oblivious and don't realize they are being passed. If they do notice, it's worse: they're willfully interfering with the race, whether out of pride or simple failure of conscientiousness. It happened a lot in that race, and in many that followed. Farthest behind was Courtney Smith of Harvard. She was run ragged, nowhere near chasing distance of the second-to-last runner. Yet as she pushed on to the finish she met chants of "Har-vard! Har-vard!" at each section she passed. It was the kind of moment you only get in track, and maybe only in Eugene. It was time for a Beer Run.

I met Katie and our friend Lindsey out on the turf, where fans without tickets or fans having a beer (no drinks allowed in the stadium) could watch the meet on a giant screen in the hot sun. We sat on the artificial field and watched the women's long jump, the little black balls of reused rubber sticking to the sweat on our hands and legs. Of all the ways we expose ourselves to toxins, replacing a grass field with an artificial one in the middle of the grass seed capital of the world has to be among the dumbest.

But the beer was good and Brittney Reese was soaring to a new meet record in the long jump, making her the second-best jumper in American history, second only to Jackie Joyner-Kersee, who would soon present Reese with her medal.

Back in the media tribune, I was confronted with my second great puzzle of the meet when Jeremy Wariner pulled up in the 400m semifinal and accepted a gracious career-acknowledging standing ovation from the fans of Hayward. I looked to my left and right to confirm that I was the only member of the press clapping. Why? The same thing had happened the night before when Sonya Richards-Ross had been unable to finish her 400m heat. Here were two great champions nearing the ends of their careers, and the very people who had spent their own careers watching them appeared unmoved. Why?

Hypothesis #1: Personal restraint. They wanted to cheer but were duty-bound by their serious responsibilities as journalists to not give anything away. Inside they were moved, only outside were they blank. But were they such good actors? And could anyone's understanding of objectivity be so naïve? No, they weren't hiding their emotions. There were no emotions to hide.

Hypothesis #2: They'd seen it all before. This was my first professional meet, it wasn't theirs. This hypothesis gathered some anecdotal support when the reporter in front of me slammed a 5-Hour Energy, seemingly without disgust, the first time I'd witnessed this particular act of self-abuse. This was a man who was clearly used to doing what the job required without regard to personal well-being. Where this hypothesis breaks down is in the interest these reporters showed in the sport itself. They were not bored, only re- moved. They knew more of the runners than I did, made ob- scure predictions, and took interest when something unex- pected happened. So they weren't exactly jaded. What then?

With Hypothesis #3 I finally got it: They did not under- stand themselves as observers of the events but as partici- pants in the show, insiders. They saw themselves as integral pieces in the meet's puzzle. Not as important as the athletes or coaches, they would concede, but not ever to be mistaken for mere fans either.

I hope I fit into this group as badly as I think I do.

That afternoon I entered a cannabis shop to buy weed legal- ly for the first time since Amsterdam. I came out with two joints of something called Atomic Bomb and a mint choc- olate edible. I hadn't smoked in some time and the stuff hit me fairly hard.

By the time I got up to Pre's Rock my high permeated my body down to where the soles of my feet touched my flip- flops. Time started to do that thing where if you forget to mind it it vanishes on you. How long had it been since I joined the crowd here to leave my finisher's medal after the Eugene Marathon? How long since I used to pass by here on runs during college? How long since Pre himself was last here, his blood spilling out over the very pavement where I now stood? How long before when a singular human be- ing became a cultural reference point, an historical idea? It was too macabre a scene, standing there educing Pre's death again. I felt a sudden and distinct impression that he de- served some privacy, and I left him to it.

Day 3

On Sunday, Katie, Lindsey, and I were strolling the grounds, leisurely finding our way to the first Beer Run of the day, when the Nike tents' offer of shade drew us in. These three tents were silver-gray hemispheres of ostentatious size and prominence. What else would you expect from Nike? The air temperature dropped about ten degrees as the diesel-powered air conditioning spilled out of the front opening. The thing we noticed in the first tent was there wasn't much in it. Some TVs around the perimeter showing, I don't know, something about running, I suppose. No one paid them any mind. In the center of the tent was a wall, on the back side of which was the history of Nike's role in U.S. track and field told in about five pairs of shoes. It was not uninteresting at all, but it was awfully meager for the high-tech balloon we were all gathered in.

A tunnel led us to the second tent. This one featured the Nike Olympic uniforms with the focus of the attention given to about five flowing rows, each row its own color, of about one hundred of the ugliest and most technologically advanced running shoes you've ever seen. We were wondering what the point of this was when a young man not identifiably associated with Nike told us there was room for three more people in the next tent. Why not? We passed through the next tunnel, and here is where things really got strange.

I turned in the third tent to examine the shoes displayed on the wall but was halted by another young man whom I could not identify as being associated with Nike, who told me I had to move in the opposite direction and that the event was about to start. The door to the previous tent closed and the lights dimmed. In the middle of the tent, on large circular platform ringed with outward-facing treadmills, the master of ceremonies took his microphone and interrogated the crowd, "Are you ready?" "Are you pumped?" and so on. The three of us didn't know what we were meant to be ready and pumped for, but the thirty others gathered seemed to, as they clapped with moderate enthusiasm. The lights were dimmed further as music played and graphics were put up on the inside of the dome in planetarium manner. The emcee shouted to be heard. Altogether too much explaining was required of him for what was conducive in the loud, dark environment, but the gist of it was this: a bunch of people would come out onto the platform and run 400m on the treadmills, attempting to keep Evan Jager's mile pace that long. It sounded like a fun challenge to me, and from the safe anonymity of the dark room I was pretty sure I could do it. The runners were brought out and were each wearing the ugly shoes from the second tent. They were given a minute or two to warm up and accustom themselves to the treadmills, which adjusted themselves to the runner's pace, instead of vice versa (thank god). It was quite dark by now and quite loud. Clearly we were meant to think we were witnessing something significant. The runners were ready. One had already discovered in warm-ups that he could run faster if he supported his bodyweight on the arm bars. The emcee was ready. "Are you ready?!" he asked again. I guessed we were. "Let's do this!" he shouted with the kind of enthusiasm that must have impressed his supervisor and earned him the job. Then, looking at his device, he added apologetically, "In just one more minute." The volume of the music was lowered and the whole tent of people stood awkwardly enjoying the air conditioning. Then—"Are you ready?!"—the minute had passed, the music was loud again, and the emcee was leading us in a ten-second countdown, and the runners were running. The arm-bar guy was cheating egregiously and doing well for himself. Two of the others ran impressively and, according to the graphic on the ceiling, nearly kept up with Jager. In the end, no one made it. The emcee, nothing left to hype, was a lesser version of himself already. "Thanks for coming," he might have said as someone behind us opened a door to the outside and all the bright light came flooding in.

My synapses were more or less shot after whatever that had been. I relaxed in my bleacher seat and jotted down only the most cursory of notes the rest of the day:

- Really impressive celebration dancing from high jumper
- Tyson Gay looks old—does he have some gray in his beard?
- When the crowd cheers so loudly for former Ducks, does it disrupt the jumpers who are mid-approach?
- Wow! Allyson Felix looked out of it at 200, even 300, great finish as everyone else fell apart and she kept getting faster
- Wonderful moment: long jumper yelling "I made the team? I made the team!"
- Reporter from RunnerSpace losing water bottles, food wrappers in the wind and only halfway trying to pick them up
- No clapping again from the reporters when Otis Davis is honored—what a bunch of dickwads

Day 4

Katie and I got up to run Pre's Trail first thing in the morning. The number of fit people, young and old alike, in Eugene all week had been remarkable, but the kinds of runners we saw on Pre's Trail were the kind you can't help but ogle when they line up in front of you at a road race. Lean, sinewy, and most of them a hell of a lot faster than us. It was little surprise, then, when a mile and a half into the four-mile bark dust loop, we saw Meb Keflezighi both casually jogging and relatively flying right at us. When we crossed paths with him again later in our run he was being tailed by another runner trying to get close enough to get him in the background of a selfie, which Twitter would later prove sort of worked out for him.

At Hayward that afternoon, everyone was waiting for Galen Rupp to make his move in the 5,000m. The way he ran in the 10,000m and the way Hayward fans had seen him run for years, it felt like a sure thing that even if he was overraced and in marathon shape he would put something special together. But as the race wound down it became clear he didn't have it in him, struggling to the finish and barely advancing to the final on time. The reporter from the University of Texas, I couldn't not notice, missed the whole thing. For ten minutes he plugged himself into social media, then with two laps remaining packed up his laptop and left the stadium.

The next race, the women's 800m final, was a hell of a thing to witness. You think about these athletes, who devote their lives to training for performances that come down to fractions of inches, hundredths of seconds, minutes of degrees. From these marginal differences come their successes, their failures, their triumphs, their disappointments, and, possibly, their legacies.

A friend of mine from Minnesota is a big fan of Brenda Martinez and had me rooting for her famous kick. Lindsey is partial to the frontrunning Alysia Montaño, and I had contracted some of her enthusiasm as well. When both runners got tripped up coming into the homestretch of what looked to me like it would be a one-two finish, it was an emotionally rending confrontation with the fickleness of results. And rending for fans. It was of another order entirely for Montaño as she cried out and carried on and collapsed her way to the finish. Her Olympic dreams possibly ended, the U.S.'s chances of medaling in Rio greatly reduced—of course the Hayward fans had another ovation in them, as long as it would take for Montaño to reach the finish and then some. You cannot sit idle when a human being lays such suffering bare before you and not be moved to reach out to her in whatever form of compassionate response is available to you. Unless you're sitting in the media tribune, apparently.

The meet was only half over, but I had to get home, back to my normal concerns and pressures. As Katie drove me to Portland, where I would catch my return flight, it occurred to me that the name Donald Trump had not passed through my mind in four days. The idyll of Eugene had come to an end for me.

DON'T BE NAÏVE

It's not cheating if everyone's doing it.
What matters is that we're all racing by the same rules,
      not what those rules are.
A race is arbitrary.
You wouldn't tell me a mile means something in and of itself;
or that HGH isn't just a particular arrangement
      of molecules in the same way water and muscle
      and bones and air are particular arrangements
      of molecules;
or that some blood isn't really blood.

Don't be naïve.
You think the old-timers didn't take every advantage
      they could get.
You think getting there first isn't the only thing that counts.
That's tradition—who wins is everything, there is nothing
      else.
I pity you.

You're a footnote. I'm all caps. You're not even a footnote.
      You're a comment at the bottom of the internet
      no one is ever going to read.
You're not clever. You're not ethical. You're resentful you
      can't do what I do. Admit it. You'd rather be me.
You'd rather sign autographs at the end of a race than sign
      your name at the end of your feeble letters of protest.

I would too.

PROTÉGÉ

Trust me, I'm on your side now as ever;
No one knows better than me what's best for you.

Remember, I found you in the rain when you were a boy
    and told your parents I would teach you how to run
    and how to be a man;
I told you the deeper truth, that I would teach you how
    to die and live again as I have in marathon in Jesus in
    perpetuity;
Have I ever let you down? Have I ever disappointed you?
    Are you not a runner? Are you not a man . . . a
    Christian man?
Have you not too been reborn in this new image?

What you are facing now is a test of your faith;
What you are hearing are lies from those who have not
    been blessed as we have been blessed, those who are
    not of our caliber;
Trust your instincts: it is petty jealousy that stains the
    faithless;
Yet we must forgive them, for they know not what they do;
But to forgive is not to be misled; the Devil sneaks in the
    dark and prods our vulnerable moments; be ever
    vigilant against evil!

My son, my one true son,
I have given you everything I have, you have given me new
    life;

I would not betray you, I would not mislead you, I would not sacrifice you, I would not ask you to sacrifice for me.

WATCHING BOSTON

How do you chase what you can't see
I wanted to ask the runners in Boston.
Patiently they might have said, faithfully.
Or perhaps they could be the ones
to explain to me that what I'm chasing
isn't out ahead of me somewhere
in the distance but the metaphor itself
that will convey what it feels like
to be behind or to feel behind
or to fear that there's a faster runner
ahead who even if I run the race of my life
I will never gain, the gap simply too wide.
You let them get too far ahead, they might say.
A marathon is long but all races are
finite. You should have pushed harder you
should have been faster you should
have been another runner. Or maybe
they'd be stoic and coach me to run
my own race—it's all any of us can do,
after all. Thank you for that, I'd tell them
if they were still there to listen, which
they wouldn't be, their own races
having already led them on toward that horizon
we're all the time chasing.

TO BE A BODY

I sit here staring through my digital window
at the sweating breathing messy world
on the other side. I want to be a body again
to puncture the screen between the world and me.
A race has two ingredients: time and space.
The recipe, the relation between them, recorded
only after the delightful improvisation of being,
an approximation.

The screen, its pixels, its flatness, its glitches, its
buffering, an approximation of an approximation
of a simulacrum of a simulacrum of
a representation of a representation of
an image of an image of the bodies
my ancestors were, the rotten flesh of death,
like the deer I passed on the side
of a central Oregon highway bloated
and baking in the summer sun,
I inhaling its putrid reality half a mile out,
I tired, I thirsty, I sunburned, I patient, I
dangerously euphoric, I still moving,
albeit slowly now, my sensations all my own.

MORNING POEM #18

Starting a run these days
is like exhuming a corpse.
These old bones crackle,
I'd say *back to life* but
they just keep on crackling,
and I just keep on moving
one crackling step after
another. What is there to
say? The body knows
only so many tricks,
their effects diminishing.
The pain shooting through
my nerves—it's the only cure
I know to calm my nerves.
My back hurts, my lungs
hurt, even my ears are
asking my legs to be quiet.
My physical-therapist sister
tells me my hips are losing
flexibility. I tell her they lost
it long ago, if they ever had
any to begin with. Burritos
and donuts and pizza and
beer are now my belly. I
know their weight well
when I run. And yet, and
yet, after all these years,
sometimes, after a few miles,

when I make it that far, my
legs start to remember things
like what it once felt like to
burn and then burn deeper
and what it felt like for feet
never to touch the ground.
To be able to move as fast
as imagination. To lose all
sense of destination, completion.
To see these notions as entirely
beside the point. To be limitless.
To find in the meat and bones of
my body the very freedom from
same. I could go on and on. I
am ready to get as mystical
about this as one can get. It
doesn't need to make sense, it
makes meaning—meaning, the thing
I'm always looking for out there
in the woods or on the city sidewalk
but never on the nihilistic treadmill.
The thing I'm always looking for
in this shaking, inflexible body.
Tired and ragged though it is,
this body, poised to continue.

ONE FOOT IN FRONT OF THE OTHER

The tireless runner believed in the approaching finish line.
The tiring runner believed in the approaching finish line.
The tiring runner believed in the receding finish line.
The tiring runner longed for the receding finish line.
The tiring human longed for the receding finish line.
The tiring human longed for the receding white line.
The tiring human longed for the receding white light.
The tiring human longed for the approaching white light.
As the tireless runner believed in the approaching finish line.

ANOTHER ONE WATCHING KIPCHOGE RUN

This time in London where it's ten a.m.
When the race starts, not three a.m. like in Montana
Where I am probably more delirious than I realize
Which I'll pay for at six when my son wakes up
Getting up to watch a marathon and ultimately
Write a poem that tries to combine two ideas
About evolution in hopes of understanding
What explains greatness because what else
Can you call what Kipchoge has been
Doing the past several years if not greatness
Maybe mastery maybe grace maybe elegance maybe
Genius he leads from the start he runs like time
The announcer keeps noting how he always looks so same
You can't tell if he ever gets tired, *It's unbelievable!*
You might want to call him a machine if not that
Machine doesn't sound like the compliment it used to
And what you want to do is compliment someone
Who so wondrously challenges your conceptions
Of what's possible—No, thank him, thank him
For showing you what a human being can do
The mind leaps at human being: the idea presents
Itself and keeps apace Kipchoge a while: *Homo sapiens*
Evolved to be distance runners; only sub-Saharan
Africans are purely *Homo sapiens* and not descendants
Of Neanderthal or *Homo erectus* ancestors; Ergo: (Ergo?)
Genetically "pure" *Homo sapiens* (such as Kipchoge?)
Will be on average the best runners we have. Maybe so.
I'm not a scientist I'm the guy sitting here smiling

At mile 24 when he makes his move and doing a little
 whoop
That I hope won't wake my son as my awe annihilates my
 ideas
Why I ask myself when the race is over does greatness need
To be explained when it can be witnessed at three a.m.
Or now it's after five and my son will be up soon
And I wonder when he's older what we'll have learned
About what it means to be human and how we'll remember
 today

ON ED CAESER'S *TWO HOURS:*
THE QUEST TO RUN THE IMPOSSIBLE MARATHON

BEFORE ROGER BANNISTER'S 3:59.4 IN 1954 it was a serious question whether it was possible for a human being to run a mile in under four minutes. Six-plus decades later, the record, held by Hicham El Guerrouj, stands at 3:43.13, and thousands of men have bettered Bannister's time.

We won't know that the two-hour marathon is another false limit until someone breaks it, but as the world record drops closer and closer to that celestial mark the breakthrough race takes on a sense of inevitability. Dennis Kimetto, who holds the record at 2:02.57, would need to cut only seven seconds per mile to get down to the two-hour time—which sounds reasonable until you remember he's already running 4:42 pace. Then you start to wonder about the possible limits of human potential.

What it will take for someone to reach the threshold is what Ed Caesar tries to determine in his book *Two Hours*. Centering on the story of Geoffrey Mutai, one of the all-time great marathoners, Caesar explores the psychology, physiology, history, and culture of the distance to inspiring effect. The list of variables he considers includes foot structure, muscle fiber, surface area of lungs, altitude of youth, societal work ethic, personality, shoe technology, composition of running surface, weather conditions, and some I'm surely forgetting.

The best chance of a two-hour marathon, Caesar argues, will be a matter of placing the right runners in the right environment, one specifically designed for peak performance, rather than a city marathon (even a flat one like Berlin or Chicago), where race tactics and conditions often hinder overall speed.

Another important factor will be drawing as much talent into the pool of marathoners as possible. Because of the positive-feedback loop of Kenyan marathon success, that country does a good job of identifying and developing its running talent. In the U.S., where running is mostly a pastime of wealthy hobbyists, and competitive racing is essentially invisible, who knows how much potential is unrealized.

Whether we want to establish the institutions it would take to produce a generation of great American runners who can compete with the Kenyans is a tough question. And the best recommendation for it, to my mind, is what it can feel like for a runner to achieve excellence.

Here's Ceasar's account of Mutai taking the lead for good in the 2013 New York City Marathon: "The Spirit coursed through him. 'I didn't notice anyone,' he would say afterward, and looking at him, you could believe it. There was no thought of world records, course records, goals, demons, splits. He did not think of the next race or the runners who were behind him. It was just him, alone, on Fifth Avenue. He had become the workings of his own body."

A worthy goal for any runner.

ON THE EVE OF KIPCHOGE'S TWO HOURS

What must it have been like to witness
Bannister or Bikila or Beamon or Bolt?
I like the words *imagination* and *possibility*
when they're coupled with, say, *exploded*
which is how a younger me classified
Bolt, who he randomly saw break
the 100m world record for the first time
May 31, 2008

I was flipping through channels waiting
for my sister to get dressed for the run
we were about to go out for along the bluffs
of North Portland above the river when I saw
eight men crouched like a line of stones
I waited with them—   and then:
9.72

When it was over I thought no way how lucky
was that and who is this guy like is he for real
or what and what was his name again? Bolt?
Have you heard the thing about last names
Like how if your name is Dennis your odds
Of becoming a dentist are statistically greater
Than random? My sister comes downstairs
Our last name means keeper of the parks
And we are both fast but nothing exceptional
We go out that morning and the river is glistening
A bit more perfectly and the birds are singing a bit

Prettier and the trees are a little bit greener
And Portland is full of flowers a little bit sweeter
Than they were an hour ago and now it's 2019
And my sister's knee doesn't allow her to run much
And I'm older and slower than I used to be and
Everyone who is born one day will die
And the universe itself will eventually burn
Or freeze and in the very heart of it all
Kipchoge is running tonight
I'll be watching and I expect
My imagination will explode
What I think possibility means will explode
And I tell you if you read this in time
To watch it too because it matters
So much it means so much it matters everything
Right now

ALMOST

didn't go for that run
this morning in the rain
& missed the chance
to get wet & go fast
& feel strong & see
drops splatter on the river
& three deer still
as statues by the path
& geese in my way
& I in theirs until
I yielded—
what a shame
it would have been
not to have had the chance
to yield

WHY I RUN

In running I try to give order to my messy life,
Take all the whirligigging of my psyche and channel it into
    a refined and easy stride,
To bring the whole of my nature to bear on one graceful
    moment,
To unite all the cross purposes of myself into one
    concentrated I,
One being willing this single and ancient act of movement
    through time and space.

Running is sacred if anything is sacred,
And running I discover . . . again . . . again . . . again . . . the
    sacred in me.

Do you see me? Does my stride appear effortless?
Do I appear as I am   sacred—in my effortlessness?
And is not effort equally human, equally sacred, as
    effortlessness?

We are feelings, and feelings are facts.

Sometimes I make no effort, and sometimes

I do.

DEDUCTION ON THE RUN

Reflexive axiom of running: A runner is one who runs. (The being is in the doing.)

Evolutionary axiom of running: The human body was made to run. (Absence of telos does not indicate absence of purpose.)

Dynamic conclusion: Running, one becomes what one is.

Author's commentary: Running is a joy. (Joy, the feeling of realizing one's possibilities.) The runner represents a high point for the human being. (Q.E.D.)

GEAR UP

FLIPPING THROUGH A STACK OF *Runner's World*s this morning, I was struck fresh by the quantity and sophistication of all the running-adjacent products advertised and modeled and reviewed and mentioned and endorsed and fetishized in the magazine's glossy pages, almost none of which are useful, let alone necessary, for the simplest and most instinctual physical act our species engages in this side of sex and breathing (activities for which too consumer goods abound amidst hypercapitalism).

Apologies for uglying this up with a word like *hypercapitalism,* but this subject gets me going. Running is something your body does, not something you do in order to have a reason to go shopping. The idea that there's something wrong with you that a clever marketing campaign can entice you spend hundreds of dollars to fix is the very kind of deceit running should teach us to see through. We evolved over millions of years to run and the only thing that makes running even possible now is a product that was invented two months ago?

My son is almost two and a half. He's been running for a year, since not long after he started walking. I'll tell you what my wife and I didn't do: we didn't teach him how to run, we didn't tell him he should go running, we didn't take him to the store and buy him equipment, we didn't tell him there was something wrong with his arches or his gait or his metabolism or his electrolyte balance or goodness knows what. About the only thing we did do was put him on the ground and give him room for the spontaneous and exuberant joy of being to pulse through his body down to the soles of his feet that were making their way through the world that is big and good and wonderful and that we grow out of and find our way through and enjoy if we don't forget how.

Every time I watch him run I'm reminded that I don't need anything to run my son doesn't already have. Feet, legs, energy, a sense of joviality. That's about it.

I don't need custom insoles. I don't need shoes that support or shoes that cushion. I don't, for that matter, always need shoes. I don't need compression sleeves. I don't need Kinesio tape. I have been told a hundred times to never run in cotton. I do it all the time. I don't need special foods before my run or during my run or after my run. I don't need to have a recovery plan or a training schedule. I don't need special equipment to facilitate my cool down. Frankly, I don't need a cool down. Almost anything I do after I stop running I can do while cooling down. Which reminds me I don't really warm up. I just start running and go as fast as it feels good to go for as long I feel like going. I don't write any of my runs down in a special notebook or post them on a "social" "media" site. I don't want anything electronic around when I'm running. I have enough of that every other waking moment of my life. A run is like a shower for me: my thoughts are my own there.

I can wander on a run from the dumbness of running consumerism to an acknowledgement that I'm drawn to some of the consumer products and that sometimes I even buy them before remembering they don't do much for me, and in the end I might wander back to my boy and how happy he is when he's running and how he runs when he's happy and how if you're watching him you can't always tell which is the cause and which is the effect or if this is one of those virtuous feedback loops that are the stuff of beauty.

MINDLESS RUNNING

ONE OF THE UNDERAPPRECIATED PLEASURES of running has to be the pure mindlessness of so much of it. Once you understand that your body knows what to do when it's running the mind no longer has to be made to hover over it like some petty shift supervisor. Relieved of its normal responsibilities—or let us say *habits*—the mind is free to wander as whimsically as it pleases, following this thought and that one, wondering about this or that possibility, unburdened by logic or likelihood. And doesn't the mind sometimes on a run more like tune out, turn off, and float away somewhere while the rest of you goes about the essential business of putting one foot in front of the other.

But whether wandering or resting (and by all means, let's agree to let the mind choose for itself), the mind tends to open up creatively. As a writer, I have two reliable ways of surprising myself on the page. One is to load up on caffeine until the very brink of a mania and see if I can write coherently before I start shaking too much to type. The other is to go for a run. But crucially I do not run *in order* to figure something out on the page, which would be like swallowing a bitter vitamin rather than eating a juicy piece of fruit. I run because it's a thrill. And the thrill is as mental as it is physical. Speaking of fruit, that's what ideas grow like when I run. Half of them fall to the ground along the way and decompose before they have a chance to be documented. I find the loss itself a blessing. After all, I can't hang onto everything and I may as well not torment myself by trying to. If I were to save all my fruits from spoiling I'd have to carry a refrigerator on my back, which I don't have to tell you is no way to run.

Does language make us human? It is what allows us not only to communicate but to represent symbolically, and it is this representing that allows us to abstract from experience.

There is no abstraction in running. It is the rare and unfortunate runner who is too much in his own head during a run. Maybe runners are too often in their own heads when they're not running and this is part of why they run, but during the run language becomes less a mechanism of distancing than a decoration of experience. Language might go on being generated, but there is no seriousness about it. The center of identity drifts on a run away from the mind toward the body, and so what the mind may do is largely its own business. It is decidedly harder to suffer when we are not identified with our thoughts.

But if language makes us human, does disidentifying with it make us less human or more? I don't know. And before proceeding to speculate let me declare that it hardly matters. What matters to a runner is the running and what it feels like and what it means. The rest—how running works on body and mind, how we are evolved to run, which causes produce which effects—backed or not by science, are intellectual pursuits for idle moments, just as good as scratching an itch. My own feeling is that running makes me more human. An anthropologist might tell me it's because I'm living my evolutionary purpose when I run. A physical therapist might say it's because I sat too long this morning at my desk. I accept both happily. But I respond, mindlessly, even stupidly, that whether or not my ancestors ran and whether or not I sit too much, running makes me happy.

I could end the essay there and have said all that needs to be said. But another word on language and happiness might be added, for when my thoughts have their strongest purchase on me I often experience myself as a tool of theirs rather than they of mine. Running, I'm often able to reverse this relationship. That is, it allows me to say what I want to. Or at least get closer.

RUNNING IS MY THERAPY

You hear people say sometimes
I know what they mean
I tell my therapist one morning
You are yourself when you run
And whoever you are is okay
You accept yourself, she says
In a way that makes me think
We aren't talking about runners
In general but the one sitting
On this couch in pink Nikes
Acknowledging the pronouns
Are all wrong, that those *you*s
Really should be *I*s if it is okay
For me to be myself here
Halfway into a conversation
That is imagined not reported
Trying to communicate openly
And honestly with you or her
About the feet-on-the-ground fact
That I don't know what people mean
When they say running is their therapy
I know only what I mean when I say
I run, imagining it can't be far off,
Noticing that I'm not crying yet
& while the conversation is imagined
The therapist is as real as I am
Her office adjacent the cow pasture
That is the best place to run in our town

So whether running is my therapy
Or therapy is my therapy running
Is where I go after therapy to practice—
Paraphrasing Nietzsche or my therapist
Or the history of evolution in my legs—
The congruence of becoming who I am

ON MARK ROWLANDS'S *RUNNING*
WITH THE PACK: THOUGHTS FROM THE ROAD
ON MEANING AND MORTALITY

GO TO YOUR LOCAL PARK and notice the runners. If you watch carefully you'll be able to distinguish between those who are running to accomplish something (calorie burning, usually) and those who are running because they love it. Initially you might think it's the fast ones, those who are "good" at running who enjoy it most, but if there's a correlation here it's not causal. Plenty of slow runners love it as much or more than their more gifted compatriots.

Mark Rowlands, for instance, is an undistinguished runner. (I'm not being rude here: "I suppose the most important and obvious fact about me as a distance runner is this: I am not very good at it.") Nevertheless, Rowlands enjoys running and is able to appreciate in it, as he describes in *Running with the Pack: Thoughts from the Road on Meaning and Mortality*, the important distinction between instrumental and intrinsic value. It's in the terms of this distinction that he goes about building his case for the place of running in a flourishing human life.

Rowlands identifies in contemporary society an obsession with utilitarian, efficient, productive—in short, instrumental—values, that distances us from the joys that are available to lives that participate regularly in intrinsic value. That he proposes running to provide such intrinsic value puts him at odds with the reasons many runners run: doing work that pays off. But for Rowlands, "At its best, and its most valuable, running is play not work." The kinds of evolutionary reasons that make this so have received significant attention over the past several years, especially thanks to the book *Born to Run*. The way Rowlands puts it: "The inescapable conclusion seems to be that our modern sedentary life is one for which we have not been designed and for which, at least biologically, we are poorly equipped.... We are happiest and healthiest when we live our history, and so become what we are." For him, our status as embodied creatures has everything to do with the kinds of values that are accessible to us.

Intrinsic value and running—the marketing team at Pegasus must have wondered whether to present *Running with the Pack* as a running book for philosophers or as a philosophy book for runners. According to online buying patterns, readers are thinking in the latter terms and placing it in the company of books on the thoughtful end of the running spectrum. Given this categorization, it makes sense when Rowlands provides basic definitions of concepts that will be easily familiar to readers of philosophy. As a book, then, that is meant to popularize philosophy as well as to show that it is grounded in an activity as pedestrian (pun intended) as running, Rowlands takes the usual shots at academic philosophers for not asking the right questions. ("People sometimes ask—this is after all what philosophers are supposed to do, though few of us these days do it—what is the meaning of life?") This is probably a fair criticism from the perspective of the runner-reader who is concerned with the meaning of life but not with the specialized concerns of academia. However, a similar criticism then applies to Rowlands when he gets away from his central argument and spends inordinate time on love, fatherhood, and his dogs—all fine topics, but ones that appear awfully afield in this context.

That criticism aside, Rowlands is convincing with regard to the matter at hand: Running, when approached in the right way, affords an opportunity for play that is necessary for adults who spend so much pitching back and forth between work and entertainment. And one of the fortunate ironies of running is that "play is what running essentially is—and even when one runs for other, specific, reasons, play keeps continually reasserting itself at the heart of running." The instrumental value is ultimately overcome by the intrinsic.

The book itself is structured as a series of runs, with Rowlands beginning a particular run and following it where it leads, both geographically and intellectually. The tangents, then, are logical even as they distract. The repetition, though does create a rhythm that brings the reader in line with Rowlands's thoughts and creates the space for philosophical insight. A long-distance runner spends serious time attending to his or her inner life. Rowlands proves himself a philosopher when he divides and classifies stages in the runner's inner life according to the philosophies of Spinoza (mind and body in action), Descartes (dualism), Hume (selflessness), and finally Sartre (nothingness).

It's odd on first thought to put Sartre at the pinnacle of this progression, as he saw anguish "in the gap between reasons and actions." But in the same gap Rowlands sees joy, which it's the book's main aim to praise. "Joy is nothing more than the recognition of intrinsic value in life." As anyone who has finished a first marathon will know, the letdown of achieving a goal can explode the very concept of goals. As Rowlands says, "Running distance is a goal-based achievement that reveals the bankruptcy of goal-based achievement." Of course, such joys are available to non-runners as well as to runners, but running is one good way to get there.

FOR THE HELL OF IT

THERE ARE LOTS OF REASONS people run. I won't bother you by listing them. Instead, I'll get straight to the one good reason to run: for the hell of it.

This essay is what's left after deleting a much, much longer essay laying out an argument for why our distraction economy is perilous and play is essential. I deleted it because I've written that essay a time or two before, and all I really want to say here is that when you come down to it *for the hell of it* is the only good reason to do anything.

If you've ever tried to explain running to someone who doesn't do it you've likely heard yourself straining to convince the person that running is relaxing and soothing and invigorating and actually very easy once you get used to it and sometimes something like mystical and most of all a kind of expression of who you really are at your core. And you've likely noticed this other person looking back at you like you belong to a different species. Of course, the feeling is mutual.

Fine. Who cares. Leave the argument and go for a run. Unless what you really like isn't running but making pointless arguments, in which case, to each his own.

But whether or not you enjoy running, this *for the hell of it* notion is relevant. It's the only reason to do anything that can withstand even the slightest scrutiny. Let's review the situation. You will die, and for the time being you are alive. You have come out of this world, and one day you will return to it. Your consciousness allows you to overwhelm yourself with ideas about what you should do and should have done and so on with all the suffering this way of being produces. Meanwhile, there is music playing and we might be dancing.

This has nothing to do with hedonism. It isn't the base desires that a good life settles for satisfying. It is those that demand our fullest engagement, those that absorb us completely, those that energize rather than deplete us. Our values are grounded nowhere but in our values. Everything reduces to this.

You sometimes hear that such and such is (like) a marathon, meaning such and such is long. Well, what if life were like a marathon but not in the sense of being long? The joy of running a marathon comes (for the most part) with running a marathon. It is a challenging thing almost no one does for any reason other than for the hell of it. What other reason could there be to run one? And couldn't this be the way life is. It is surely a great thing to run a marathon. And just as surely it is a greater thing to bring a marathoner's attitude to the whole of one's life and one's own forms of play—to dance to the music you hear.

THE CHARACTER OF THE RUNNER

1. There is no perfection in running. Not for Bolt, not for Kipchoge, not for me, not for you.

2. Your philosophy meets the ground as you meet the ground. You encounter your limits, your frustrating embodiedness, your particularity.

3. Transcendence in running concerns conceptions, usually self-conceptions.

4. The runner answers only to himself.

5. To put yourself into situations you can't think your way out of or worry your way out of but can by some primal logic run your way out of, situations in which you are compelled by Nietzsche's claim that the mind is merely something the body does, situations in which you can feel your entire evolutionary history in your bones and muscles and the surprising ease of your breathing, these are the moments runners know to be holy.

6. We might remember that at our core, core as in what is irreducible about us, we are physical facts. We are sperm and egg joined and grown from the energy we have drawn from our environments. We are the way we are because of how prior things were: these genes, these nutrients, these conditions. And then here we are. And what are we? We are hulking masses, sweating stinking huffing puffing creatures.

7. Running brings us to our bodies. It also brings us to our *selves*. More than anything else, it teaches us who we are. It reveals our strength and our fitness. It reveals our dimensions and our realities. It discards the imagined self and replaces it with the brute fact of who we really are. It is your body out there and what you can do with it. What could be more honest?

8. There is no room for self-deceit in running. It reveals to us who, in all depth and dimensions, we are and who we are not.

9. Notice that running's freedom is born of its restrictions. The more limited it is the freer you are. It is a Zen tea ceremony in sneakers.

10. If basketball is jazz, running is a birdsong.

11. Alan Watts tells us, "There is nothing wrong with meditating just to meditate, in the same way that you listen to music just for the music. If you go to concerts to 'get culture' or to improve your mind, you will sit there as deaf as a doorpost." If we were to apply this idea to running we would say that a run is never to be endured for some other sake, it is only and ever to be run.

12. The only way to receive what running offers is to unburden it of any hopes or expectations and open yourself to the joy of the experience. Forget results. Forget speed. Forget distance. Think only of the running. Or not even that.

13. There are a few or maybe several runners who go into a marathon hoping to win. And there are often thousands who go into the same marathon hoping to set a personal record or just to have fun or maybe just to finish. With this range of abilities and expectations attends an atmosphere of camaraderie and celebration. Fans will cheer

for slow runners as for fast ones. You can be objectively not super great (as in not super fast) and still feel good about yourself and feel encouraged and supported by other runners. Commit yourself fully to play. It is its own reward.

14. You don't have to be good at something to enjoy it. It is okay to be as good as you are and no better. It is okay to not even try to be good but rather to plant yourself squarely in the center of your own experience and let it thrive there as it will. There are many activities through which this claim can be put to the test. I have always enjoyed running.

RUNNING AND TIME

with Dōgen

1. A runner running.

2. There is no flower apart from flowering. So then, where is the runner apart from running? The being is in the doing. And the doing—running just as flowering—is a creative expression.

3. Because running does not exclude running, it is running.

4. When you run the world runs through you, when you run there is nothing else to do, when you run nothing is undone.

5. The tree does what is in its nature to do. The runner recognizes the tree.

6. Alan Watts writes, "Running is not something other than myself, which I (the organism) *do*. For the organism is sometimes a running process, sometimes a standing process, sometimes a sleeping process, and so on, and in each instance the 'cause' of the behavior is the situation as a whole, the organism environment."

7. Each run is particular. A particular route with particular footfalls and original breaths amid a particular atmospheric composition, particular fitness and particular

mindset in this particular present moment we only ever know.

8. The experience of time is just like the experience of a run. The ground comes toward you and then retreats behind you. The whole time you're right where you are.

9. There is only now. If you can't be in the now now there is no other time available to you in which to do so. There is no now that comes later, only the now that is now.

10. If you run a race to get to the finish you will never arrive.

11. However, if you run right where you are you can go anywhere.

12. One thing to be said for running hard is that it forces you into the now. Things are happening fast enough, requiring enough of your attention, that you are engaged with your surroundings. You are connected to your environment. You always are, but we forget this oftentimes to our own detriment. Running brings us back to the world.

13. Run without running. If you can run without making any effort you will discover that no effort is required of you and that you can run indefinitely without tiring. If instead you strain to run you will find yourself never able to give as much (go as far, go as fast) as you'd like. You will be tired from the time you start till the time you quit.

14. Trust yourself. Trust your body. Trust your legs. Trust your breathing. You will meet runners who have doubts about what they can do and these doubts become their limitations. Similarly, you will meet runners who are confident they will accomplish some great feat and injure themselves straight away. If you trust your body

you can listen to it and let reality (rather than your ideas about it) determine what you can do.

15. A race is a measurement. It measures what you are capable of on a given day. There is no particular meaning to the result. It could have been more or less, faster or slower, but is only what it is: a result. And because there is no meaning, there is no pride and no shame. On one part of this planet a certain human being ran a certain distance in a certain time. Let us visit this race, and let us notice that nearby a flower is blooming. As it blooms it takes no stock of another flower that is perhaps larger or brighter or more symmetrical or a closer approximation of the Platonic flower. Let us bring our runner back to this flower in a few months' time and ask him to notice that now the flower is wilting and that in its wilting it feels no shame, does not cling to its appearance from a few months prior. Let us ask our runner to reflect. Let us ask this of ourselves. And when we are satisfied, let us go out for a run and run until it is appropriate to stop.

www.ingramcontent.com/pod-product-compliance
Lightning Source LLC
Chambersburg PA
CBHW020940090426
42736CB00010B/1203